The Astrology of Nations is a master class in mundane astrology and a new classic for an emerging generation of astrologers and astrological magicians. True to the accessible style of JMG's esoteric oeuvre, this text is informative, important, and a joy to read. It takes its place among the most-significant volumes of the astrological art and should no doubt occupy a similar position on the bookshelves of both novice and expert practitioners."

—Ike Baker, author of *A Formless Fire: Rediscovering the Magical Traditions of the West* (2024, Tria Prima Press) and host of the ARCANVM podcast and YouTube channel

THE
ASTROLOGY
of Nations

CASTING AND INTERPERTING CHARTS FOR
NATIONS, POLITICS, AND ECONOMIES

JOHN MICHAEL GREER

JOHN MICHAEL GREER

THE
ASTROLOGY
of Nations

CASTING AND INTERPERTING CHARTS FOR
NATIONS, POLITICS, AND ECONOMIES

REDFeather™
MIND | BODY | SPIRIT

4880 Lower Valley Road, Atglen, PA 19310

Library of Congress Control Number: 2024941286

Designed by Alexa Harris
Cover design by Brenda McCallum
Type set in Bodoni/Baskerville

ISBN: 978-0-7643-6874-5
ePub: 978-1-5073-0526-3
Printed in China

Published by REDFeather Mind, Body, Spirit
An imprint of Schiffer Publishing, Ltd.
4880 Lower Valley Road
Atglen, PA 19310
Phone: (610) 593-1777; Fax: (610) 593-2002
Email: Info@redfeathermbs.com
Web: www.redfeathermbs.com

For our complete selection of fine books on this and related subjects, please visit our website at www.redfeathermbs.com. You may also write for a free catalog.

REDFeather Mind, Body, Spirit's titles are available at special discounts for bulk purchases for sales promotions or premiums. Special editions, including personalized covers, corporate imprints, and excerpts, can be created in large quantities for special needs. For more information, contact the publisher.

We are always looking for people to write books on new and related subjects. If you have an idea for a book, please contact us at proposals@schifferbooks.com.

CONTENTS

PART 1

THE ART OF MUNDANE ASTROLOGY

CHAPTER 1

INTRODUCING MUNDANE ASTROLOGY

Astrology is a complex field with many different branches. Mundane astrology, which makes predictions about the political and economic condition of nations, is one of those branches. Despite the obvious importance of its subject matter—who doesn't want to know in advance about the political and economic future of the nation they live in?—it has been relatively neglected over the last century or so. Recently, however, astrologers in many countries have begun to revive the classic techniques of mundane astrology and put them to use.

Like every branch of the ancient science of the stars, mundane astrology requires a firm grasp of the basics of astrological science. This first chapter will attempt to provide that. If you already know your way around natal astrology—the most popular branch of astrology, the one that deals with individual birth charts—you will find some things about mundane astrology very familiar and others very strange. If you don't know a thing about astrology yet, don't worry—this book will provide you with everything you need to know.

DEFINITIONS

Let's begin with a few definitions, so everyone is clear on what is being discussed.

Astrology is the empirical science and craft of the correlations between planetary movements and human affairs. Its earliest surviving records date from more than five thousand years ago in valleys of the Tigris and the Euphrates Rivers, in what is now Iraq. The scholars of several ancient cultures in that area hypothesized that there might be connections between events here on Earth and the observed movements of the Sun, Moon, and planets, and they started keeping records in an effort to find out what those connections might be.

That was, as scientists nowadays like to say, a fruitful hypothesis. By 1600 BCE, astrologers were making detailed predictions based on the patterns their forebears had observed. By 600 BCE, horoscopes in the modern sense of the word had come into use. Greek, Roman, Arabic, and Persian scholars in the centuries that followed made their own contributions to astrology. So did the astrologers of medieval and Renaissance Europe, and of course the same thing is true of every corner of the modern world as well. Astrology today remains an active, evolving field full of ongoing research and lively disputes.

Mundane astrology is the oldest branch of astrology, the one that analyzes and predicts political and economic trends on the basis of planetary movements. The kind of astrology that most people think of first, the astrology of individual personality and destiny as shown in birth charts, is called *natal astrology* or, if you prefer a more old-fashioned term, *genethliac astrology*. There are several other branches of astrology: horary or divinatory astrology, which answers specific questions; electional astrology, which determines the most auspicious time to begin an action or new project; medical astrology, which assists in the diagnosis and treatment of illnesses; and others.

While they share a basic theoretical structure and many other features in common, each branch of astrology has its own tools and techniques, which have evolved over the centuries as astrologers checked their charts and predictions against events. Keep this in mind, because one common mistake of the inexperienced is trying to use the techniques of natal astrology in mundane work. Mundane charts are cast in the same way as natal charts, but their delineation—that is, the analysis of factors and their synthesis into a complete picture—follows different rules.

The planets are the main active indicators in astrology. The word "planets" in ancient Greek literally means "wanderers," and in earlier times it stood for every visible object that moves noticeably against the background of the stars. Later on, scientists divided things up further. Astrologers who want to be precise these days speak of the Sun and Moon as "luminaries," and Mercury, Venus, Mars, Jupiter, Saturn, Uranus, and Neptune as "planets." (The dwarf planets Ceres, Pluto, and Eris, along with an assortment of smaller bodies, belong in a different category; we'll get to them a little later.) Each planet has a distinctive influence on human affairs, and the condition and relationships of each planet in relation to the whole chart can be used to predict how things will turn out here on Earth.

No, nobody knows why. In astrology we're in the position of people who lived before the time of modern physics, who knew that rocks fall when you drop them, but couldn't tell you why that happens. This is why I described astrology as an empirical science. We don't know the mechanism by which astrological effects work, and given the prejudices of modern science, it's unlikely that we'll get funding for the necessary studies any time soon. The fact that the cause is unknown, however, doesn't keep the effect from being real. Did rocks fall any differently before Isaac Newton figured out the laws of gravity?

Benefic planets are generally favorable indications, and *malefic planets* are generally unfavorable. The Moon, Venus, and Jupiter are benefic, while Mars, Saturn, Uranus, and (in mundane charts, though not more generally) Neptune are malefic. Mercury is variable—he can be benefic or malefic depending on context—while the Sun is generally benefic but acts like a malefic when in conjunction with other planets. A planet conjunct the Sun is termed *combust*, and that means just what it looks like: the energies of the planet are burned up by the Sun, metaphorically speaking, and have very little effect.

There are also two belts of smaller objects in the solar system: the asteroid belt between Mars and Jupiter and the Kuiper Belt out beyond Neptune. An important share of the research and disputation mentioned above have to do with the role that asteroids and Kuiper Belt objects (KBOs) play in astrology. One worldlet in the asteroid belt, Ceres, is large enough that scientists class it as a dwarf planet, and at least two of the KBOs, Pluto and Eris, fall into the same category; their importance in astrological charts is hotly disputed. Some astrologers also work with the larger asteroids; with a small, icy body named Chiron, which orbits between Saturn and Uranus; and with theoretical planets such as Vulcan and Lilith—I have not found any of these to produce good predictions in mundane astrology, but others may get different results.

The signs of the zodiac are 30° wedges of the zodiac—the band of the sky through which the planets move, as seen from Earth. Each sign has a symbol and a name and is associated with one of the four traditional elements—Fire, Earth, Air, and Water—and with one of three modalities, also known as modes or qualities—cardinal, fixed, and mutable. The elements are easy to understand if you treat them as metaphors, and tradition assigns qualities to each element to help with this: fire is hot and dry; earth, cold and dry; air, hot and moist; and water, cold and moist.

The modalities are also easy to understand because they have to do with qualities of action: the influence of cardinal signs tends to come on strong and fade out quickly, that of fixed signs is stable and difficult to budge, and that of mutable signs is elusive, changeable, and tricky.

SIGN	MEANING	ELEMENT	MODALITY	RULER
♈ Aries	Ram	Fire	Cardinal	Mars
♉ Taurus	Bull	Earth	Fixed	Venus
♊ Gemini	Twins	Air	Mutable	Mercury
♋ Cancer	Crab	Water	Cardinal	Moon
♌ Leo	Lion	Fire	Fixed	Sun
♍ Virgo	Virgin	Earth	Mutable	Mercury
♎ Libra	Balance	Air	Cardinal	Venus
♏ Scorpio	Scorpion	Water	Fixed	Mars
♐ Sagittarius	Archer	Fire	Mutable	Jupiter
♑ Capricorn	Goat	Earth	Cardinal	Saturn
♒ Aquarius	Water-carrier	Air	Fixed	Uranus
♓ Pisces	Fishes	Water	Mutable	Neptune

The signs of the zodiac and their meanings, elements, modalities, and rulers

The signs of the zodiac are not the same as the constellations—thus, for example, the group of stars labeled Aries is not the same as the zodiacal sign Aries. (In ancient times, the constellations used to be in the signs, which is where the confusion comes from.) The signs are regions of space counted from the point in the heavens where the Sun is located at the moment of the spring equinox. That's 0°♈, which is pronounced "zero degrees Aries." Measure 30° around the ecliptic in the direction the Sun moves, and you're at 0°♉, "zero degrees Taurus," and so on around the sky.

All this refers to what is technically known as *tropical astrology*—no, that has nothing to do with casting charts under a palm tree with a piña colada in hand! It gets its name from the tropic (from the Greek word for "turning") lines on the earth and in the heavens, which mark where the Sun finishes its apparent northward or southward motions over the course of the year and turns to go the other direction. There is also another school, called *sidereal astrology*, which anchors the signs to the stars rather than the Sun and thus puts them in different parts of the sky. In the Western world, at least, sidereal astrology is much less widely used than tropical astrology, and in my experience the forms of it practiced in the Western world don't yield accurate predictions in mundane work. That said, there are some astrologers who swear by it.

There is also Vedic astrology, also known as Jyotish, the astrological tradition of the Indian subcontinent. It is a sidereal system rather than a tropical system, but it has its own very different ways of interpreting the heavens. It works very well, and I've been interested to note that sidereal

Vedic mundane predictions and tropical Western mundane predictions tend to parallel each other closely, despite the differences in the methods. The maps are not the same, but the territory obviously is! That said, I don't practice Vedic astrology; if you want to study it, you need to read a book by someone who does.

Dignity and *debility* are the astrological terms for the strength or weakness of planets. A planet that is dignified has a stronger or more positive influence than usual, and the aspects of human affairs that it represents will share in that strength or positivity. A planet that is debilitated has a weaker or more negative influence than usual, and the aspects of human affairs that it represents will share in that weakness or negativity. There are two kinds of dignity and debility. Essential dignity or debility comes from the planet's placement in the zodiac, while accidental dignity or debility comes from the planet's placement in the houses, and from the aspects between planets (we'll get to houses and aspects shortly).

SIGN	OPPOSITE SIGN
Aries	Libra
Taurus	Scorpio
Gemini	Sagittarius
Cancer	Capricorn
Leo	Aquarius
Virgo	Pisces
Libra	Aries
Scorpio	Taurus
Sagittarius	Gemini
Capricorn	Cancer
Aquarius	Leo
Pisces	Virgo

The zodiac signs and their opposites

Rulership, detriment, exaltation, and *fall* are relationships that the planets have to the signs of the zodiac. Every planet rules one or two signs and is exalted in one sign. When a planet is in the sign opposite to one it rules, it is in its detriment, and when it is in the sign opposite to the sign of its exaltation, it is in its fall. These are crucial in mundane astrology because they have a potent effect on planetary dignity and debility. When a planet is in its rulership, it is strongly dignified. When it is in its exaltation, it is well dignified, and the things it rules also tend to take on unusually positive or constructive forms. When it is in its detriment, it is strongly debilitated, and when it is in its fall, it is debilitated and the things it rules also tend to take on unusually negative or destructive forms. The table below shows these relationships:

PLANET	RULERSHIP	EXALTATION	DETRIMENT	FALL
☉ Sun	Leo	Aries	Aquarius	Libra
☽ Moon	Cancer	Taurus	Capricorn	Scorpio
☿ Mercury	Gemini & Virgo	Virgo	Sagittarius & Pisces	Pisces
♀ Venus	Taurus & Libra	Pisces	Aries & Scorpio	Virgo
♂ Mars	Aries & Scorpio	Capricorn	Taurus & Libra	Cancer
♃ Jupiter	Sagittarius	Cancer	Gemini	Capricorn
♄ Saturn	Capricorn	Libra	Cancer	Aries
♅ Uranus	Aquarius	Scorpio	Leo	Taurus
♆ Neptune	Pisces	Gemini	Virgo	Sagittarius

Relationship of planets to the signs of the zodiac

The exaltations and falls of Uranus and Neptune are still being debated, since both these planets were discovered in recent centuries, and research is still continuing on their astrological properties. I use the dignities and debilities worked out by twentieth-century astrologer Ivy Goldstein-Jacobson, whose work generally informs my astrological practice.

Triplicity, face, and *term* are minor dignities that the planets receive from certain areas in the zodiac. I use them in some of my charts, but they're a refinement best added after you have some experience with the major dignities. The triplicities, faces, and terms of Uranus and Neptune have not yet been determined, though research is ongoing.

For the other planets, there are three sets of triplicities: day, night, and mixed; a planet gets dignity in its day triplicity when the Sun is above the horizon, in its night triplicity when the Sun is below the horizon, and in its mixed triplicity at any time. There are several versions of which planet has what triplicity. The set I use is known as Dorothean, after the Greek astrological writer who first introduced them in ancient times.

Each of the faces, also known as decans, is 10° wide or one-third of a sign. The first one runs from 0° to 9°59'59" (that's "9 degrees, 53 minutes, 59 seconds" if you say it aloud) of a sign, the second from 10° to 19°59'59", and the third from 20° to 29°59'59". Each one has its own planetary ruler; again, there are several schemes for assigning rulers to faces. The triplicities and faces I use are as follows.

SIGN	"DAY TRIPLICITY"	"NIGHT TRIPLICITY"	"MIXED TRIPLICITY"
Aries	Sun	Jupiter	Saturn
Taurus	Venus	Moon	Mars
Gemini	Saturn	Mercury	Jupiter
Cancer	Venus	Mars	Moon
Leo	Sun	Jupiter	Saturn
Virgo	Venus	Moon	Mars
Libra	Saturn	Mercury	Jupiter
Scorpio	Venus	Mars	Moon
Sagittarius	Sun	Jupiter	Saturn
Capricorn	Venus	Moon	Mars
Aquarius	Saturn	Mercury	Jupiter
Pisces	Venus	Mars	Moon

The triplicities for each zodiac sign

SIGN	"FIRST FACE"	"SECOND FACE"	"THIRD FACE"
Aries	Mars	Sun	Venus
Taurus	Mercury	Moon	Saturn
Gemini	Jupiter	Mars	Sun
Cancer	Venus	Mercury	Moon
Leo	Saturn	Jupiter	Mars
Virgo	Sun	Venus	Mercury
Libra	Moon	Saturn	Jupiter
Scorpio	Mars	Sun	Venus
Sagittarius	Mercury	Moon	Saturn
Capricorn	Jupiter	Mars	Sun
Aquarius	Venus	Mercury	Moon
Pisces	Saturn	Jupiter	Mars

The faces, or decans, of each zodiac sign

The terms I use—the Ptolemaic terms, to give them their proper name—are as follows:

♈ ARIES	Jupiter 0°–5°59′	Venus 6°–13°59′	Mercury 14°–20°59′	Mars 21°–25°59′	Saturn 26°–29°59′
♉ TAURUS	Venus 0°–7°59′	Mercury 8°–14°59′	Jupiter 15°–21°59′	Saturn 22°–25°59′	Mars 26°–29°59′
♊ GEMINI	Mercury 0°–6°59′	Jupiter 7°–13°59′	Venus 14°–20°59′	Saturn 21°–24°59′	Mars 25°–29°59′
♋ CANCER	Mars 0°–5°59′	Jupiter 6°–12°59′	Mercury 13°–19°59′	Venus 20°–26°59′	Saturn 27°–29°59′
♌ LEO	Saturn 0°–5°59′	Mercury 6°–12°59′	Venus 13°–18°59′	Jupiter 19°–24°59′	Mars 25°–29°59′
♍ VIRGO	Mercury 0°–6°59′	Venus 7°–12°59′	Jupiter 13°–17°59′	Saturn 18°–23°59′	Mars 24°–29°59′
♎ LIBRA	Saturn 0°–5°59′	Venus 6°–10°59′	Jupiter 11°–18°59′	Mercury 19°–23°59′	Mars 24°–29°59′
♏ SCORPIO	Mars 0°–5°59′	Jupiter 6°–13°59′	Venus 14°–20°59′	Mercury 21°–26°59′	Saturn 27°–29°59′
♐ SAGITTARIUS	Jupiter 0°–7°59′	Venus 8°–13°59′	Mercury 14°–18°59′	Saturn 19°–24°59′	Mars 25°–29°59′
♑ CAPRICORN	Venus 0°–5°59′	Mercury 6°–11°59′	Jupiter 12°–18°59′	Mars 19°–24°59′	Saturn 25°–29°59′
♒ AQUARIUS	Saturn 0°–5°59′	Mercury 6°–11°59′	Venus 12°–19°59′	Jupiter 20°–24°59′	Mars 25°–29°59′
♓ PISCES	Venus 0°–7°59′	Jupiter 8°–13°59′	Mercury 14°–23°59′	Mars 24°–25°59′	Saturn 26°29°59′

The planetary rulers of the faces for each zodiac sign

A planet is *peregrine* if it's in a part of the zodiac where it has no dignities at all. This counts as a debility. Another debility worth noting is *retrogradation*; a planet is retrograde when it appears to be going backward when seen from the standpoint of the Earth. (It's not actually going backward, of course; the effect is produced by the relative positions and motions of the Earth and the other planet.)

Aspects are geometrical relationships between planets as seen from the surface of the Earth. When two planets are in aspect, the things they rule are related, and the nature of the relationships can be read from the nature of the aspect. The major aspects are these:

ASPECT	DEGREES	NATURE
Conjunction	0°	Mixed
Sextile	60°	Helpful
Square	90°	Hostile
Trine	120°	Helpful
Opposition	180°	Hostile

The planetary aspects

A helpful aspect means that the phenomena indicated by the two planets help and strengthen each other, while a hostile aspect means that they struggle against and weaken each other. A conjunction is mixed because it depends on the planet. A conjunction with a benefic planet is helpful, and one with a malefic planet is hostile. Yes, this means that when a malefic planet is conjunct with a benefic one, the malefic benefits and the benefic suffers!

The *orb* of the aspect is the wiggle room within which the aspect is considered effective. This varies dramatically from one branch of astrology to another—for example, many natal astrologers give very wide orbs to major aspects, while some other branches of astrology give only very narrow ones. Mundane astrology falls somewhere in the middle.

In a mundane chart, when the Sun or Moon is involved, the orb for conjunction, square, trine, and opposition is 8° to either side—so, for example, if the Sun is at 0°♈ and Saturn is between 22°♍ and 8°♎, they are in opposition. When the aspect is between planets other than the luminaries, the orb for a major aspect is 5° to each side—so, for example, if Venus is at 20°♋ and Jupiter is between 15°♓ and 25°♓, they are in trine. In any case, the more exact an aspect is—in astrological jargon, the closer it is to perfection—the stronger it is, and the further from perfection it is, the weaker it is. Toward the edge of the orb, the weakness becomes serious; a planetary aspect more than 3° distant can be too weak to play an active role, depending on the dignities or debilities of the planets involved.

There are a great many minor aspects. Most of them are too weak to provide a basis for accurate predictions in mundane charts and so are best ignored. Three of the minor aspects, however, can play a significant role in mundane charts:

ASPECT	DEGREES	NATURE
Semisquare	45°	Hostile
Sesquisquare	135°	Hostile
Inconjunct	150°	Hostile

The minor planetary aspects

Give these aspects an orb of 5° when a luminary is involved, and 3° otherwise.

The *houses* are twelve areas of the heavens as seen from a particular spot on the Earth's surface at a particular moment. Each house relates to a different department of human affairs. These departments are complex and important enough that we will be discussing them in detail a little later on in this chapter. There are various ways to calculate the houses, and yes, I've tried many of them. I find that the Placidus system works best for me in mundane charts, as well as in other forms of astrological work.

The *angles* are the ascendant, midheaven, descendant, and nadir. At the moment for which the chart is cast, the ascendant is the point of the zodiac rising on the eastern horizon, the midheaven is the point highest above the horizon, the descendant is the point setting on the western horizon, and the nadir is the point farthest beneath the horizon. Most house systems, including the Placidus system I use, treat these as boundaries of houses. Planets that are approaching the angles as the sky turns are called *angular*; this is an important accidental dignity. Points that are just past them are called *cadent*, from a word meaning "falling"; this is an important accidental debility.

THE ASTROLOGICAL CHART

With all this in mind, let's move on to the basic working tool of the astrologer, the astrological chart. You'll find an example that follows: the 2019 Aries ingress chart for Washington, DC. You may find it useful to bookmark this page, because the material that follows will make much more sense if you can follow along and study the details of the chart as we go.

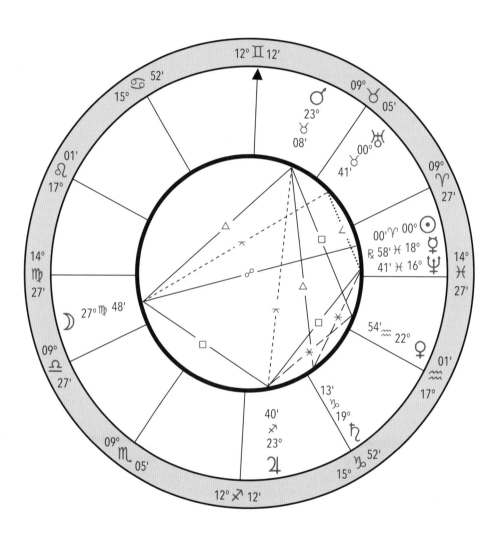

The 2019 Aries ingress chart for Washington, DC

An astrological chart is a schematic diagram of the heavens as observed from a particular position on Earth at a particular moment. In the example chart, the horizontal line that runs from 14°27' Virgo to 14°27' Pisces is the horizon; 14°27' Virgo is the ascendant in this chart, as well as the cusp of the 1st house; and 14°27' Pisces is the descendant, as well as the cusp of the 7th house. The houses run counterclockwise around the sky, so houses 1–6 are below the horizon and houses 7–12 are above the horizon. Yes, the 1st house in this chart is the one with the Moon in it, and the 7th house is the one with the Sun, Mercury, and Neptune in it.

The arrow at the top of the chart, pointing to 12°12' Gemini, is the midheaven and the cusp of the 10th house; the line opposite it, which ends at 12°12' Sagittarius, is the nadir and the cusp of the 4th house. As explained above, the ascendant, midheaven, descendant, and nadir are the four angles of the chart. Between each pair of angles are two more house cusps, calculated according to the house system you use: in the case of this chart, the Placidus system. Each cusp has its position in the zodiac marked on it.

In this chart, each of the twelve signs of the zodiac has a cusp in it. *This does not always happen.* In some charts you'll have houses wide enough that an entire sign fits inside with room to spare on either end, so that it has no cusp in it. When that happens, the sign and any planets in the sign are said to be *intercepted*; this is a debility, and it means that whatever the planet represents is unable to act freely and suffers from restrictions and limitations. This doesn't happen in charts drawn up using what's called the whole-sign house system, an ancient system that has become popular in some circles today. That's why I don't use that system: intercepted signs and planets can give you crucial information about events to come.

Take a moment to think back from the chart to the actual experience of the heavens. Imagine that you're standing in Washington, DC, just before six o'clock in the evening on March 20, 2019. You're facing south; the Sun is setting off to the west, and although you can't see them, Mercury and Neptune are setting just ahead of him. Mars and Uranus are high in the southwestern sky, while Venus, Saturn, and Jupiter are below the Earth from where you stand; they're shining down from the night sky at this same moment in China. Off to the east, the Moon is still below the horizon from where you stand, but she'll rise in a little under an hour (it takes four minutes on average for the ascendant to change by 1 degree). Do this shift of the imagination from time to time with astrological charts, and it will help you keep in mind that what you're looking at isn't a bunch of abstract squiggles on paper, but the glory of the heavens themselves, as observed from the place and time that interests you.

Got it? Excellent. At this point we'll move on to what is far and away the most important thing you need to learn in order to make sense of mundane astrology: the meanings of the houses. Understand what the houses mean and, just as crucially, what they don't mean, and you can make sense of a mundane chart and use it to make accurate predictions. Lose track of the houses and their meanings, and you're lost in space with no way home. Most of the disastrously wrong mundane astrology predictions of recent years—and there have been some howlers—have been so badly mistaken because the people who made them forgot to notice which houses were influenced by the planetary events they were looking at.

The meanings of the houses that follow, by the way, are specific to mundane astrology. Natal astrology also uses houses, and many natal astrologers use the same Placidus house system I do, but they give the houses a set of interpretations relevant to natal charts, which are *not* the interpretations relevant to mundane charts. This is one of the places where you can really mess things up by trying to use natal techniques to interpret a mundane chart.

These are the standard meanings of the twelve houses in a mundane chart:

1st house: This house represents the ordinary people of the nation, especially those members of the population who have no effective voice in the political process—that is to say, despite the usual rhetoric of modern politics, most of us. It shows the general condition, prosperity, health, and attitudes of the masses.

2nd house: This is the house of the national economy—specifically, the productive economy, which generates goods and services for consumers, as distinct from the speculative economy, which generates unearned wealth, which belongs to the 5th house. All the ordinary ups and downs of economic behavior can be read here, and so can changes in taxation and the budget of the nation's government.

3rd house: This house deals with the internal transportation, communications, and media of the nation, including the internet, and all the economic sectors related to these things. The condition of this house indicates the condition of all industries that have to do with these sectors of the economy, from auto manufacturers to social media firms. It also governs the public schools, and primary and secondary education, but not the universities, which belong to the 9th house. It can also indicate the nation's relationships with the nations with which it shares land borders or very close sea borders—for example, charts for England, France, and Belgium can be indicated by the 3rd house.

4th house: This house relates to agriculture, mining, and other resource industries, and anything else underground. It also rules real estate and its value, as well as the condition of the rural hinterlands of the nation and of its rural population. This is also the house that governs the political party or parties out of power at the time the chart takes effect.

5th house: This house is the house of speculative finance, gambling, tourism, the entertainment industry, professional sports, celebrities, and the rich and famous generally. It also governs the upper house of the national legislature, in nations that have two legislative houses—for example, it represents the Senate in charts cast for the United States, and the House of Lords in charts cast for Great Britain.

6th house: This house governs the state of public health, epidemics, and disease generally. It also rules the condition of the nation's labor force, the interests of the working classes, and also the state of the nation's armed forces and of the national civil service.

These first six houses all deal with the practical foundations of national life. In my mundane delineations I refer to them collectively as the economic hemisphere, as distinct from the remaining six houses, which are the political hemisphere.

7th house: This is the house of foreign affairs, the place in a mundane chart where you are most likely to find peace, war, power politics, international incidents, and political treaties (but not trade treaties—those belong to the next house). Every kind of political interaction between different nations belongs here, and so does the foreign policies of the nation for which the chart is cast.

8th house: This house governs foreign trade and investment, trade and economic treaties, and every other form of economic exchange between nations. This is also traditionally the house of death, and so the deaths of leading politicians and increases in the national death rate can be signaled by this house.

9th house: This house governs what seems at first like a curious grab bag of topics. It is the house of the national judiciary, and especially of the nation's highest court. It is the house of religion, and especially of the established religion of the nation, if there is one. It is the house of universities and higher education. It also governs maritime affairs, air travel, and space travel. Finally, it is the house that rules astrology. All these make sense if you simply remember that 9th-house affairs always relate to what is high above or far away: abstract ideals such as justice, theological entities such as gods, the vast distances covered by space travel, and so on. This is where a nation reaches into the distance.

10th house: This is the house of the executive branch of the national government, though the head of government has a different representation in the chart, as will be explained shortly. It represents the power and authority of the government and the nation as a whole. It also governs the party in power at the time the chart takes effect.

11th house: This is the house of the national legislature, and specifically of the lower house of the legislature if the nation has two legislative houses— the House of Representatives in the United States, for example, and the House of Commons in Great Britain. It rules laws and the processes by which they are passed and repealed.

12th house: This house represents the institutions of national life—its hospitals and prisons, but also its nongovernmental organizations, its nonprofit sector, and its voluntary organizations. It also rules the nation's intelligence agencies, its criminal underworld, and all secret things.

These are the twelve basic categories into which the entire collective life of a nation fits. Take some time to think about them: to figure out which of them relate to any randomly chosen news story, for example. Notice that houses that are opposite each other form a polarized pair: the 1st house of the national population pairs with the 7th house of relations with other countries, the 2nd house of the domestic economy with the 8th house of foreign trade and investment, and so on. Get used to the houses. Once you know one thing further about them, they become the key that opens up the meaning of a mundane chart.

Here is the one thing further that you need to know. Ready?

The condition of the planet that rules each house, modified by the nature and condition of any planets in that house, reveals the condition of the affairs of that house for the period indicated by the chart.

Memorize those words, or at least be absolutely sure you've grasped the concept. You'll thank me later, because this is the key to traditional mundane astrology.

How do you tell which planet rules a given house? That depends on the sign that rules the cusp of the house. You learned about planetary rulerships earlier in this chapter—this is where that knowledge becomes crucial. Let's say you want to know how a nation's economy will behave during the period indicated by a mundane chart. So you look at the second house—do this now with the example chart—and you find the zodiacal sign Libra on the cusp. Libra is ruled by the planet Venus, and so you look at Venus. There she is, over in the 6th house. Her position is 22°54' Aquarius, and she's peregrine in that part of Aquarius—that's a debility. She is square the malefic planet Mars, which is a strong debility, but she receives help via a sextile with the benefic planet Jupiter, which is a significant dignity.

She has another debility, however, because of the house where she is located. Remember the discussion of angular and cadent planets? That is judged by house. A planet in the 1st, 4th, 7th, or 10th houses is angular, and thus stronger than usual. A planet in the 3rd, 6th, 9th, or 12th houses is cadent, and thus weaker than usual. Because she is placed in the cadent 6th house, Venus is weak, and when added to her other debilities that makes her decidedly weak, though in better condition than she might be due to the sextile with Jupiter.

That gives you a first glance at the state of the economy during the period governed by this chart. It's only a first glance, because the 6th house is more than just a place for a planet to be cadent—it tells you that issues related to public health or the workforce, or both, are likely to be involved in the condition of the economy during the period in question. It's only a first glance, because Mars and Jupiter aren't simply a minus and a plus: each of them has its own condition and house rulership to take into account, and these and their interpretations also have to be brought into the picture. Still, once you understand that the planet ruling each house is an indicator of the condition of that house's affairs, you have the key to the mundane chart, and most of the other complexities of mundane astrology become clear if you keep a good tight grip on that key.

Do the planets also have their own meanings, irrespective of their role as surrogates for the houses? Yes, and those meanings are also very important to take into account. Two of them are especially important in mundane charts:

The Sun in a mundane chart is the indicator of the head of the government: the president in the United States, the prime minister in Great Britain and the countries of the Commonwealth, and so on. The Sun's condition and aspects in the chart tell you what the head of government is likely to do, and what is likely to happen to him or her.

The Moon in a mundane chart is the indicator of the people—more specifically, of the politically active classes, the minority of the population that has the wealth and influence to take an active role in shaping the political discourse. The Moon's condition and aspects tell you what the politically active classes are likely to do and experience, while the relationship between the Moon and the planet that rules the 1st house tells you about the relationship between the politically active classes and the rest of the population.

The other planets also have traditional attributions, which can be used to illuminate what is going on in a mundane chart. I have found that certain changes to the traditional assignments make for more-accurate predictions.

Mercury in a mundane chart represents the nation's intellectuals, its chattering classes, talking heads, media figures, and vendors of ready-made opinions. It also provides another look at the state of its media, transport methods, and educational system.

Venus in a mundane chart represents the nation's women and the women's vote, and **Mars** in a mundane chart represents the nation's men and the men's vote. When the old textbooks of mundane astrology were written, the roles available to women in society were tightly circumscribed, and so it made sense to assign women to Venus and tacitly assume that all the other categories were occupied by men. We live in a different era; there are still a recognizable women's vote and a women's political culture, but a corresponding men's vote and a masculine political culture are emerging to balance it. The relation between the men's vote and the military, the old meaning of Mars in mundane charts, is still close enough these days not to matter in practice.

Jupiter in a mundane chart represents the nation's corporations and corporate culture, including both for-profit and nonprofit corporations. In earlier eras, when established religious bureaucracies were a major political force, Jupiter was the planet of institutional religion, but here again, we live in a different era. I have found that Jupiter is a good indicator of the role of the corporate sector in modern political and economic life.

Saturn in a mundane chart represents the rural and small-town population, and the political and social force of the hinterlands. It is also a good indication of the retiree vote, a powerful force in many countries these days.

When mundane astrology was developed, Saturn was the farthest planet known by astronomers and astrologers alike. The discoveries of Uranus in 1781 and Neptune in 1846 launched an exciting era of research and experimentation for astrologers. It takes a long time to sort out the meaning of a newly discovered planet, especially if that planet moves very slowly through the zodiac. The role of these two planets in mundane astrology is still being worked out in detail, though the basic outlines are clear. The following attributions are those I use.

Uranus is the planet of the individual, and in a mundane chart he represents those small groups of people who have a disproportionate role in shaping national life. He represents the national legislature, the inner circles of influential politicians, innovators, creative minorities, dissident subcultures, and conspiracies. He also indicates all those who transgress traditional boundaries, and is thus the planet of alternative sexualities and of gender identities outside the usual dichotomy of male and female.

Neptune is the planet of unities. He governs all mass phenomena, and in a mundane chart he represents those trends and forces that emerge out of the majority of people who are shut out from the influential classes and given only a nominal role in the political process. He shows the interests and opinions of the people as a whole, and also those political movements such as populism that rise out of the populace and embody its goals.

In historical astrology, Uranus and Neptune represent influences that have only recently come into manifestation in human consciousness. This explains their late discovery compared to the other planets. At present, and for centuries to come, we are still sorting out the contending pressures of these two planetary influences: between the Uranian concept of individual liberty and the Neptunian concept of universal equality, for example. Since both influences are still not well integrated, Uranian influence often takes the role of eccentricity, Neptunian influence often takes on the role of delusion, and both planets tend to function as malefics in terms of ordinary political and economic life.

Notice also that the planets fall neatly into a set of binary pairs, with one exception. Sun and Moon define the binary between the ruler and the rest of the political class; Venus and Mars, the binary between women and men; Jupiter and Saturn, the binary between urban corporate culture and the rural hinterlands; Uranus and Neptune, the binary between the individual and humanity in the mass. Mercury, the elusive androgyne planet, evades assignment to any of these binaries and takes on different relations to each planet as he moves through different aspects.

By this point, if you've been paying attention, you're probably about to make a wholly reflexive attempt to lunge through the pages of this book, grab me by the shoulders, and shake me until my teeth rattle, shouting, "But all this means that a single planet can mean many different things!" That's quite correct. In fact, a single planet can mean quite a number of things: first, because Mercury, Venus, and Mars rule more than one sign, and second, because a single sign can sprawl across more than one house cusp. That's one of the things that makes astrology complex.

An astrological chart is a matrix of meaning in which the signs, planets, and houses come together to create intricate patterns that have to be interpreted in a range of ways, with a galaxy of nuances added in for fun. You can't simply analyze it in an "A equals B" manner; in fact, even the most complex analysis will get you only halfway there. The other half is synthesis—and the practice of astrology is one of the best ways yet discovered for learning to work with these two paired functions of the human mind.

One of the great challenges of astrology, in turn, is that analysis is relatively easy to teach, but synthesis is a knack that has to be learned. The one way that astrologers have found that leads to learning it is close attention to many charts. This leads to the next issue that must be confronted, because the charts that reveal the political and economic future of a community or a country are not the ones commonly used in today's popular natal astrology. It is to this, and to certain other barriers in the way of effective mundane practice, that we now turn.

CHAPTER 2

THE CHARTS THAT MATTER

The first chapter of this book has covered the basics of astrology in general: what it is, what raw materials it uses, and how it assembles those into the astrological chart, the basic working tool of the astrologer. I've presented these from the perspective of mundane astrology in particular, exploring what the planets and houses mean when they are applied to nations and communities rather than, say, the lives of individuals. The same basic ingredients of the chart, however—the planets, the signs, the houses, the dignities and debilities, and so on—are used by most other kinds of traditional Western astrology as well.

You might think, since this is the case, that it would be easy for people with a solid background in other kinds of astrology to make the leap to mundane work and produce accurate predictions of political and economic events. Unfortunately that hasn't been the case as often as one would like, because of the overwhelming focus on natal astrology over the last three quarters of a century. Early in the twentieth century, that wasn't true, and a wide range of different branches of astrology saw significant work done. When astrology became fashionable in the 1960s, by contrast, natal astrology was the only branch most people wanted to hear about, and not just because "So, what's your sign?" quickly became one of the standard pickup lines in singles bars.

We live in an egocentric age. A great many people these days have been taught to treat their feelings, their cravings, and the other transitory antics of their personalities as the pivot around which the whole universe spins. People in the grip of that kind of egomania love to hear all about themselves.

27

Since astrologers need to pay their bills like everyone else, natal astrology thus became the be-all and end-all of the art.

This has several downsides from a mundane perspective. To begin with, a background in natal astrology can lead astrologers to give too much emphasis to minor factors and pay too little attention to the major ones. There are valid reasons for attention to minor factors in natal charts. If you focus your astrological work on exploring personality, it's important to include even the most subtle and minor influence, because it's precisely these easy-to-miss factors that can make a natal delineation so revealing.

In any form of astrology that focuses on prediction, by contrast, it's more important to treat the minor factors as minor and the major factors as major. This is particularly true in mundane astrology, where a subtle and minor influence will reliably have a subtle and minor effect—quite possibly too subtle and minor to be visible in the hurly-burly of political and economic events. The main tendencies of the future will be shown by the primary factors of the chart—above all, by the condition and relationships of the planets ruling or placed in each house of the chart.

The word "tendencies" is important here, because mundane astrology—like every kind of astrological prediction—deals in probabilities, not certainties. There is an old maxim that says, "The stars incline; they do not compel." This is always worth keeping in mind. A mundane chart doesn't tell you what's going to happen; it tells you what's likely to happen and what pressures are exerting their influence on what will happen. Since statistical tendencies tend to work out more reliably when many people are involved, mundane astrology is very often quite accurate, but it's always wisest to state your predictions as probabilities rather than flat statements. Those who don't do this can embarrass themselves when events take unexpected turns.

These are honest mistakes. Another common source of trouble in mundane astrology is more problematic. There are unfortunately some people who dabble in mundane astrology in order to use it as a way to get the heavens to tell them and their readers or clients what they want to hear, rather than listening to what the heavens actually have to say.

Now of course that bad habit has been a problem since the invention of soothsaying far back in the childhood of our species. It's just as pervasive now as it was in the days when the Roman writer Cicero wondered in one of his essays how diviners could pass each other in the street without bursting out into laughter. Those of my readers who have done divination for paying clients, as I have, know just how large a share of the clients are interested only in being told that the universe is their pet poodle and will infallibly give them everything they think they want.

Political passions being as intense as they are, mundane astrologers face the same pressure when they make their predictions. Thus it is crucial, as you begin to examine and delineate mundane charts, that you set aside your preferences and prejudices about what you think *ought to* happen or *shouldn't* happen, and see what the heavens have to say about what *will* happen. The habit of overemphasizing minor factors in a chart is a significant risk here, since it's almost always possible to find something or other that favors the outcome you want. This is why it's essential, if you want to make accurate predictions, to focus on the major indications and not let yourself be distracted by minor ones.

It's just as essential to look back over your predictions after time has passed, to see what you got wrong as well as what you got right. This is an embarrassingly uncommon habit these days. Many readers will remember the lurid prophecies of imminent utopia or doom that were churned out in gargantuan volume in the run-up to December 21, 2012. It was interesting, in a certain bleak sense, to watch how many of these would-be prophets promptly forgot all about their predictions when that date passed without incident.

As a mundane astrologer, you will be making predictions that some people may use as the basis for significant life decisions. Thus it's essential that you pay attention to the accuracy of your predictions and adjust your techniques accordingly. If you were learning archery, you'd put a great deal of attention into which shots hit the bull's-eye and which shots missed the target completely! The same willingness to correct for past mistakes and learn from your results is just as important for the competent mundane astrologer.

All these are important factors. Yet, there's another difficulty in the way of competent mundane astrology, and it's a matter of choosing the right charts to cast. The modern overemphasis on natal astrology is again to blame here, because it leads a great many people to assume that if you want to know about politics, you find some equivalent of a birth chart and interpret that.

As a result, if you read websites that talk about political astrology, you'll find that many of them talk about the natal charts of heads of state, the foundation charts of countries, and every so often the inauguration chart for a head of state, as though these are the charts that matter. It's all natal astrology, all the time, and it very often yields inaccurate predictions. Natal charts for heads of state, to begin with, are poor predictors of political events: the fact that Barack Obama amassed a large fortune during his two presidential terms, for example, doesn't mean that the rest of us were so lucky during the same period, and 1865 was a very bad year for Abraham Lincoln but a very good year for the United States.

Foundation charts and inauguration charts are more useful than the natal charts of heads of state as guides to the destiny of nations. Foundation charts are, in effect, the natal charts of entire countries, while inauguration charts are the natal chart of the administration of a president or the reign of a monarch. They have value, but they are not as central to mundane practice as current habits might suggest. Two inauguration charts and two foundation charts will be discussed in the case studies and predictions later in this book, to show some of the potentials of charts of this type. Other types of charts, however, are of greater importance to the mundane astrologer.

The charts that have been central to mundane practice for the last few millennia are less familiar, even to many practicing astrologers. They have an interesting factor in common: they are not determined by events on Earth in the way that natal, foundation, and inauguration charts are. Their timing depends on events in the heavens. We'll go through them one at a time.

SOLAR-INGRESS CHARTS

The solar ingress is the fundamental working tool of classic mundane astrology, the basic chart that has been used for millennia by mundane astrologers to track the ebb and flow of political and economic change. It's had an undeservedly negative reputation since the famous British astrologer C. E. O. Carter published his book *Political Astrology*, which lambasted the ingress chart as an inaccurate tool.

Carter's negative attitude toward ingress charts was quite understandable, since he made a fool of himself in the spring of 1939 by relying on an ingress chart to make a prediction that war would not break out that year. That failure, however, was not the fault of the ingress chart; as we'll see in the first of the case studies later in this book, the 1939 Aries ingress chart for London contained clear indications of a serious risk of war, which he ignored for certain highly dubious reasons of his own. (He also relied on a Pluto aspect, which in my experience is a very reliable way to make bad predictions. We'll discuss that, too, in a later chapter.)

It's high time to set aside Carter's sour grapes, because the solar-ingress chart deserves its traditional reputation as the workhorse of the mundane art. An ingress, in astrological terms, is the movement of a planet into a new sign of the zodiac. The ingresses that matter in mundane astrology are the ingresses of the Sun into the four cardinal signs—Aries, Cancer, Libra, and Capricorn—which mark the starting points of the four seasons of the year (the Aries ingress is traditionally the most important, since it marks the beginning of the astrological year). To cast an ingress chart for any nation, you erect a chart for the moment of ingress as seen from the capital of the nation, and interpret that using the tools outlined in the previous chapter.

One detail that needs to be remembered in order to use ingress charts effectively is that they have effect for varying lengths of time. The rising sign in the ingress determines how long the period of effect will be. When interpreting an Aries ingress, if a cardinal sign (Aries, Cancer, Libra, or Capricorn) rises, the chart will be effective for only three months, until the upcoming Cancer ingress at the summer solstice. If a mutable sign (Gemini, Virgo, Sagittarius, or Pisces) rises, the chart will be effective for six months, until the Libra ingress following. Only if a fixed sign (Taurus, Leo, Scorpio, or Aquarius) rises will the chart be effective for an entire year, until the next Aries ingress.

This same rule applies in a certain sense for the other three ingresses, but there's a catch: each Aries ingress wipes the slate clean, since it marks the beginning of a new astrological year. Thus the longest period a Cancer ingress can have effect is nine months; a Libra ingress can at most govern six months, and you don't even need to bother checking the rising sign of a Capricorn ingress, because it will have effect for three months no matter what sign is rising.

What happens if you have an Aries ingress that is in effect for an entire year? In that case the other three ingresses modify the indications of the Aries ingress. The same is true any time one ingress is still in effect when another takes place. It's entirely possible, by the time you get to a Capricorn ingress, to have the Aries, Cancer, and Libra ingresses still in effect. In that case the Aries ingress is the most important, the Cancer ingress modifies its indications, the Libra ingress adds another set of modifications to both, and the Capricorn ingress has a minor but noticeable effect on top. Yes, this can be very challenging to interpret. That's one of the things that makes mundane astrology so fascinating and complex a subject.

What about other ingresses? In traditional mundane astrology they saw very little use. It has become popular in recent years to analyze history by way of the ingresses of outer planets into the signs of the zodiac, and some very interesting analyses have resulted from this. As this branch of astrological research continues, it's quite possible that powerful mundane techniques will be developed using these ingresses. As yet, though, the jury is still out on whether the current ventures along these lines can provide accurate assessments of current political and economic trends and their likely outcomes—and that, again, is the point of mundane practice.

LUNATIONS

If solar ingresses provide the hour hand on the clock of political and economic destiny, lunations are the minute hand. The lunation is the new moon, and a lunation chart is cast for the capital of a nation for the moment of exact conjunction between Sun and Moon. These charts have effect for one lunar month each, until the next new moon.

When you are interpreting a lunation chart, always compare the positions of the planets and house cusps to the corresponding points into whichever ingress chart or charts are currently in effect. A lunation chart that has no relationship to a current ingress chart normally indicates minor events only, but if the lunation chart has strong aspects to positions in the ingress chart, it can indicate the timing of events shown in the ingress chart. This is especially true when the conjoined Sun and Moon are conjunct, are opposite, or square an important planet or house cusp in the ingress chart. This might as well be a flashing red light and a loud siren indicating that something important is about to happen (the gentler aspects, trines and sextiles, and the minor aspects don't have so potent a significance).

Some mundane astrologers also cast charts for the full moon, the exact opposition between Sun and Moon. These seem to be less significant than new moon charts but may be worth studying as a way to get a more precise focus on political or economic changes. A full-moon chart also lasts for one lunar month, until the next full moon.

ECLIPSES

One of the wild cards of the mundane deck, eclipses have been tracked systematically for thousands of years. There are of course two types of eclipses, solar and lunar. A solar eclipse is a new moon in which the Sun and Moon happen to be at the same declination—that is, distance north or south of the ecliptic—as well as the same degree of the zodiac, and so the Sun casts the shadow of the Moon onto the Earth, blotting out the sunlight from some part of the earth's surface (think of it as a hypernew moon). A lunar eclipse is a full moon in which the Sun and Moon are at the opposite declination when they are also in opposite degrees of the zodiac, and the Sun therefore casts the Earth's shadow onto the Moon, blotting out the Moon when seen from Earth (think of it as a hyperfull moon).

Both of these are traditionally negative signs, promising serious disruptions of various kinds. In both cases, the amount of disruption is measured by the degree to which the Sun or Moon is blotted out when seen from Earth. A total eclipse, in which the whole Sun or the whole Moon is obscured, indicates the most-serious consequences, but even a very modest partial eclipse warns of trouble. In either case, the chart is cast for the moment of conjunction or opposition between Sun and Moon—not for the moment of maximum obscuration, which is what the media usually reports. Astrologers who use computers to calculate their charts simply aim for the new or full moon to get the right moment; those who do things the old-fashioned way and calculate the chart by using an ephemeris—yes, they still exist!—simply look up the moment of conjunction or opposition in the monthly aspectarian.

The period of time governed by an eclipse chart is determined by the length of time the eclipse itself lasts. A solar eclipse is effective astrologically for as many years, or fractions thereof, as the eclipse lasts for hours, or fractions thereof. (You can work out the fractions by remembering that in the solar-eclipse scale, 5 minutes of eclipse time equals one month of effect, and 10 seconds of eclipse time equals one day of effect.) A lunar eclipse is effective astrologically for as many months, or fractions thereof, as the eclipse lasts for hours, or fractions thereof. (In the lunar-eclipse scale, 2 minutes of eclipse time equals one day of effect. Don't mix these scales up!) In any case, erect a chart for the moment of conjunction or opposition, for the capital of the nation you have in mind. This is interpreted like any other mundane chart, except that the Sun and Moon are always treated as being seriously debilitated, since an eclipse is the worst debility known to mundane astrology.

Two traditional rules are worth mentioning here. The first is that the effects of an eclipse are said to be strongest where the eclipse itself is visible, and weaker where it is not. I have found this to be quite accurate. The second rule claims that an eclipse affects primarily those countries that, according to traditional astrological lore, are assigned to the sign of the zodiac in which the eclipse takes place. There are lengthy lists assigning countries and cities to signs, but I have tested this rule repeatedly and I have found it to be unreliable at best. You may have different luck, however, and the tables of signs and nations can be found in most standard books on mundane astrology.

MAJOR CONJUNCTIONS

If ingresses are hour hands and lunations are minute hands, the conjunctions of the outer planets—those farther out than Earth from the Sun—are the pages of the calendar. In ancient times the conjunctions of Mars and Jupiter, Mars and Saturn, and Jupiter and Saturn were studied closely. In recent centuries, the discoveries of Uranus and Neptune have added much more raw material for such studies, though centuries of further work will probably be required before astrologers know for certain what to expect when these two slow-moving planets are involved in conjunctions.

The conjunctions of Mars and Jupiter are associated with economic troubles, religious unrest, and disturbances of the peace. The conjunctions of Mars and Saturn are associated with wars, revolutions, mass violence, and the collapse of governments. The conjunctions of Mars and Uranus are associated with major political crises but seem to be less violent an indication than the Mars-Saturn conjunction. The conjunctions of Mars and Neptune lead to "extraordinary popular delusions and the madness of crowds." Since Mars takes a little over two years to complete its journey around the zodiac, all these happen quite often.

The conjunctions of Jupiter and Saturn, which are called *great conjunctions*, happen every twenty years and are held to mark significant shifts in world history. In traditional astrological jargon the planets Jupiter and Saturn are known as the Chronocrators—literally, the Time Lords (fans of the *Doctor Who* series may make of this what they will). In traditional mundane astrology the cycle of great conjunctions sets the rhythm of human history. Due to the ratio between the orbital periods of these two planets, these conjunctions take place for many years in a row in zodiacal signs ruled by the same traditional element. Thus the 1842 conjunction took place in Capricorn, the 1861 conjunction in Virgo, the 1881 conjunction in Taurus, and the 1901 conjunction in Capricorn again—all Earth signs.

At intervals of a little less than 200 years, the conjunctions of Jupiter and Saturn change elements. There is often a little back and forth between the two elements—for example, the 1782 conjunction, like all the others for a century and a half previously, was in a Fire sign. The 1802 conjunction was in the Earth sign Virgo, the 1821 conjunction was back in the Fire sign Aries, and then 1842's conjunction in Capricorn marked the definite beginning of an Earth cycle. The conjunction that marks the definite beginning of a new elemental cycle, such as 1842, is called a *grand mutation*, because it marks the change (in Latin, *mutatio*) from one element to another.

The conjunction of Jupiter and Saturn on December 21, 2020, was such a grand mutation. The Earth cycle ran unbroken from 1842 to the 1961 conjunction in Capricorn; in 1980 and 1981, Jupiter and Saturn had a triple conjunction, caused by the planets' retrograde cycles in the Air sign Libra; 2000 saw a brief return to Earth with a conjunction in Taurus. The 2020 conjunction in Aquarius begins an Air cycle that will continue until 2219, when a conjunction in Scorpio marks the beginning of the coming Water cycle.

The cycle of great conjunctions goes all the way around the zodiac every 800 years or so. When Jupiter conjoins Saturn in the early degrees of Aries, that marks a *greatest conjunction*, the end of one era of history and the beginning of another. There are on average three greatest conjunctions in an age of the world. According to one set of calculations—as usual in astrology, there are many of these, and fierce disputes among their supporters— the Piscean Age began in 280 BCE and ended in 1879. During that age, there were greatest conjunctions in 114, 908, and 1702. These ushered in respectively the Roman era, the medieval era, and the industrial era.

The conjunctions of Jupiter and Saturn with Uranus and Neptune, and the conjunctions of Uranus and Neptune with each other, are as yet poorly understood, and much more work will be needed before they can be used as a firm basis for predictions. In general, Jupiter-Uranus conjunctions seem to reset the political and economic imagination of humanity, inspiring new goals and ideals for which people then strive, while Jupiter-Neptune conjunctions have a similar impact on the religious dimension of life and on the collective imagination more generally. Saturn-Uranus conjunctions are explosive, bringing about the shattering of outworn forms and heightening tensions between progressive and conservative factions in societies, while Saturn-Neptune conjunctions are profound and subtle, marking deep changes in the basic frameworks of human society. As for Uranus-Neptune conjunctions, those happen so rarely that the jury's still out on their effects; one hypothesis is that a conjunction between the planet of individuality and the planet of unity marks changes in the collective definition of what it means to be human. Much more research will need to be done so confirm all these indications, however.

Conjunctions may be challenging to interpret, but casting a chart for a conjunction is straightforward. The time to use is the moment of perfect conjunction, and for mundane purposes, the capital of the nation you have in mind is the appropriate place.

COMETS

Another wild card, and another branch of mundane astrology that will require much more research, is the mundane astrology of comets. The traditional lore considers them to be major malefic indications, predicting wars, plagues, and disasters, but their exact prefigurations are poorly described in the documents we have. The time at which they first become visible to the naked eye is the usual time to use for a cometary chart, and the comet is placed in the degree of the zodiac it occupies at that time. As it passes through an arc of the zodiac, the aspects it makes with the planets foretell its effects. The larger and brighter the comet, the more significant it is as a warning of trouble to come.

FOUNDATION AND INAUGURATION CHARTS

These are the two classes of standard mundane charts that are not determined by events in the heavens. The foundation of a new nation is an astrologically important moment, and it offers useful indications concerning the character and history of the nation. With nations founded in the last century or so, it is usually easy to find the exact time, date, and place of their foundation, but the further back in history you go, the more difficult this can become. As we will see in one of the case studies later on, the correct foundation chart of the United States has been a matter of some dispute for many years.

Inauguration charts also vary in their exactness. In some nations, such as the United States, the inaugural date of the new head of state is specified in the national constitution, and it is usually not too hard to find the time from contemporaneous news reports. In the case of current events, of course, you can just watch or listen to a live broadcast of the event and make a note of the time. In other countries, it can be more challenging. Given an accurate time and date, however, it is usually possible to calculate a meaningful chart. Note, however, that when a nation has a head of state who is different from the head of government—for example, Great Britain, where the king or queen is the head of state but the prime minister is the head of government—

inaugural charts for the head of state seem to be much more accurate than those for the head of government. More research will be needed to sort this out, however.

Since foundation and inauguration charts are simply variations on the basic natal-chart template, natal techniques can be applied to them with more success than to ingresses and other classic mundane charts. One natal technique that appears to offer particular promise is secondary progression. Progressed charts are a standard tool for prediction used by many natal astrologers to determine when the potentials foretold in a natal chart will become active.

Progression seems to work equally well for foundation charts. I have cast and interpreted progressed charts based on the United States foundation charts and find them to be a useful source of insights. This is another area in which more research is certainly needed. Readers who are interested in exploring this aspect of the mundane astrologer's craft will need to look up progressed-chart techniques elsewhere, however, since progression is a process all its own and, like mundane astrology itself, has distinctive requirements and methods.

A NOTE ON ASTROLOGY PROGRAMS

The varying branches of astrology differ in just how much accuracy they require. Some forms of astrological practice work best with planetary and house cusp positions that can be calculated to within a second or so of arc, and from time to time, questions have been raised in astrological forums online as to whether any given astrology program, app, or website provides the necessary degree of accuracy.

Mundane astrology, however, is among the more forgiving branches of the art. Since effective predictions depend on the most-influential factors in the chart, not on the kind of subtleties where seconds of arc make a difference, you can do a perfectly accurate ingress, eclipse, or conjunction chart if your program is accurate to the nearest degree—the kind of accuracy, that is, that was standard in the days before computers, when only the most-obsessive or most-specialized astrologers took things further than that.

If you're concerned about whether your astrology program is accurate enough for mundane purposes, there's a simple way to check. All you need is an ephemeris for the current year—that is, a book of the positions of the planets for each day of that year. Ephemerides (that's the plural) are typically drawn up for noon or midnight Greenwich time. Set your program to draw up a chart for either noon or midnight in London on any day you choose, then take the chart and compare it to the ephemeris. If the two don't match, your program (or rather the programmers who wrote it) may be bad at math.

On the off chance that it's of interest, the ephemerides I use and recommend are those issued by the Rosicrucian Fellowship, Oceanside, California. I also recommend that anyone who wants to get serious about astrology should consider learning how to cast a chart by hand, the old-fashioned way, without relying on a computer—in the process of doing this, you learn certain things about the way a chart functions that, in my experience, can be taught no other way.

I use the SolarFire astrology program for charts these days, but I have also used several others with equally good results. Remember that what was accurate enough for the astrologers of the Middle Ages and Renaissance, when mundane astrology was a lively and highly accurate art and nobody bothered with seconds of arc, is good enough for the mundane practitioner today as well.

With these points made, let's proceed now to the planets and see how each of them works in the context of mundane charts.

CHAPTER 3

─────────────────────────────────

THE SUN

In most branches of astrology, the Sun is the most important influence in the chart, and mundane astrology is no exception to this general rule. (Horary and electional astrology are among the exceptions, if you were wondering—in both of these the Moon is paramount.) Once you know the Sun's dignity or debility in a chart and apply that to the house it is in and the house or houses that it rules, you know a great deal about political conditions in the place and time covered by the chart. Add the favorable or unfavorable aspects made by the Sun to the other planets in the chart, and you have a snapshot of the conditions facing the head of government in that place and time.

If you read medieval texts on mundane astrology, you'll find that the Sun is usually treated as the significator of the monarch. That made a great deal of sense in the days when kings and queens actually had political power worth mentioning. Nowadays? It's indicative that King Charles III doesn't even get to write his own King's Speech each year; it's written for him by the party that controls the government, and he has no say in the contents. Monarchs of this common modern type are ruled by Saturn, the Lord of Time Past, not the Sun, and by the lord of the 12th house, the house of national institutions.

In modern mundane astrology, rather, the Sun represents the actual head of government—the prime minister of Great Britain and other Commonwealth countries, the president of the United States, and so on. When in doubt, assign the Sun to whichever position officially calls the shots in the executive branch of government. This is true even when the person currently filling that position is a nonentity under the control of some other politician, or of a cabal of assistants. The Sun refers to the focus of executive power, whether that power is actually wielded by the person at that focus or by others in the background. Look to the relationship between the Sun and the ruler of the

10th house, and the relative dignities of these two planets, to gauge how much power the notional head of government actually has.

The houses the Sun rules or is placed in a mundane chart indicates the department of the national life that will receive the lion's share of attention from the head of government, and from the executive branch generally, during the period for which the chart is cast. The condition of the Sun tells you how that department of the national life will affect the government and its head. The aspects the Sun makes with the planetary rulers of each of the houses provide a third level of meaning. Keep these basic rules in mind and you'll rarely go wrong.

THE SUN IN THE HOUSES

1ST HOUSE

A dignified Sun in or ruling the 1st house indicates that the head of government will be popular among the ordinary people of the nation. It very often indicates some important achievement or gain for the nation and always predicts an improvement in conditions for the people in general. Prosperity is common and public health is good if other indications agree.

A debilitated Sun in or ruling the 1st house is still favorable, because the Sun is always strong in this position. However the success or prosperity will be lessened, and over the longer term the results will be problematic. Conflict between social classes is likely and public health will suffer.

2ND HOUSE

A dignified Sun in or ruling the 2nd house is favorable for government revenue, and it also predicts improved conditions for the national currency. This is generally a favorable sign for the national economy, with improved conditions for trade and domestic industry, but it warns of relatively high government expenditures.

A debilitated Sun in or ruling the 2nd house warns of heavy government expenditure, increased taxation, and serious waste of public revenue. The national government's budget will likely be a source of trouble during this period. Depending on aspects, this can also warn that an important business or influential person is on the brink of bankruptcy.

3RD HOUSE

A dignified Sun in or ruling the 3rd house is favorable for the mass media, transportation, and communications industries. Government attention to these sectors of the economy can be expected and will have positive results;

the head of government will have an easier time than usual communicating with the people. This placement also favors primary and secondary education and makes constructive reforms in that sector likely. Finally, it favors good relations with bordering nations.

A debilitated Sun in or ruling the 3rd house predicts trouble for the nation's mass media, transportation, and communications networks. Corrupt practices or the misbehavior of leading figures in these sectors may be revealed. Problems with primary and secondary education will also come to public awareness. Relations with neighboring nations will face difficulties.

4TH HOUSE

A dignified Sun in or ruling the 4th house is favorable for agriculture and for resource industries such as mining and logging. Government policy toward these sectors of the economy will improve conditions. This placement is also favorable for real estate. Since the 4th house also stands for the party out of power, it can predict improved prospects for that party.

A debilitated Sun in or ruling the 4th house brings troubled times for agriculture through drought and unfavorable government policy and also predicts difficulties for resource industries; government policies will hinder these sectors of the economy. Real estate will perform poorly, and the party out of power will suffer.

5TH HOUSE

A dignified Sun in or ruling the 5th house is favorable for speculative markets and for the entertainment industry and predicts a pleasant and prosperous period for the nation generally, since this is the Sun's native house. Professional sports benefit from this placement. Celebrities and elite society receive favorable attention; the birthrate is likely to increase. The upper house of the national legislature, another 5th-house correspondence, will take the lead in matters important to the nation.

A debilitated Sun in or ruling the 5th house predicts troubled times for speculative markets and the entertainment industry, with lurid scandals a likely outcome for the latter. Celebrities and elite society will suffer due to missteps or scandals. Professional sports suffer, and the upper house of the legislature overreaches itself or suffers unfavorable publicity.

6TH HOUSE

A dignified Sun in or ruling the 6th house is very favorable for public health and improves conditions for the working classes, service industries, the civil service, and military personnel. Reforms of the civil service or military carried out under this influence will be successful.

A debilitated Sun in or ruling the 6th house is bad for public health, warning of fevers and other epidemic diseases. It predicts discontent among the working classes; strikes and labor actions are likely, and business interests are troubled. The civil service faces challenges. In countries at risk of military coups, this placement can be a warning of trouble of this kind.

7TH HOUSE

A dignified Sun in or ruling the 7th house brings important positive changes in foreign relations. It predicts friendship and good feeling between countries. Treaties and summit meetings are favored when this placement is in effect, and highly publicized marriages among famous people are likely. Conflicts can be resolved at this time.

A debilitated Sun in or ruling the 7th house predicts troubles and complications in interactions with other countries. Foreign relations are unsettled, and the government risks making serious mistakes in its international dealings. If other indications support this, there is a risk of war. The nation and its government will face a great deal of criticism and hostility from abroad.

8TH HOUSE

A dignified Sun in or ruling the 8th house is favorable for foreign trade and investment, and trade agreements are favored under this influence. Export industries thrive, the balance of trade improves, and foreign capital is readily available.

A debilitated Sun in or ruling the 8th house warns of troubles with foreign trade and investment. Trade agreements negotiated or enacted while this placement is in effect will have negative effects on the national economy. Export industries and the balance of trade suffers, and foreign capital is restricted or is more costly than usual. Since the 8th house rules death in natal charts, an afflicted Sun in this house can also indicate the death of an important political figure.

9TH HOUSE

A dignified Sun in or ruling the 9th house is favorable for the judicial branch of government, for higher education, and for religion. Under this placement the courts make influential decisions, the universities benefit from government action, and favorable reforms are likely in higher education or in religious matters. If the nation has a space program, it may score a significant success during this period. This placement also brings success to the nation's astrologers.

A debilitated Sun in or ruling the 9th house is less favorable for the affairs of this house. It brings undue political pressures to bear on the courts, the universities, and religious bodies and can also warn of scandals and unfavorable publicity for one or more of these. If the nation has a space program, it will be troubled, and astrologers will face difficulties.

10TH HOUSE

A dignified Sun in or ruling the 10th house is a very favorable indication for the government and the nation, promising strong and successful government and a period of good fortune for the nation. It promises personal popularity for the head of government.

A debilitated Sun in or ruling the 10th house is as unfavorable a sign as the preceding is favorable. Under this influence the government risks overreaching itself and landing in serious difficulties. Depending on other indications, the death of an important political figure may be likely.

11TH HOUSE

A dignified Sun in or ruling the 11th house is favorable for the national legislature, and especially for the lower house. It promises the passage of beneficial legislation and helpful reforms in legislative work. It strengthens the legislative branch and gives it power over the other branches of government. It also promises support from friendly nations abroad.

A debilitated Sun in or ruling the 11th house predicts quarreling and grandstanding in the national legislature, the failure of proposed legislative measures, and changes in the cabinet. Legislation is hindered or delayed, and the legislative process is disorganized. Usually friendly nations abroad will be less likely to offer support.

12TH HOUSE

A dignified Sun in or ruling the 12th house predicts success and stability for the nation's institutions. Government attention to the institutional sector will have good results. This placement is also favorable for intelligence agencies and other secret organizations, and it decreases problems with organized crime.

A debilitated Sun in or ruling the 12th house brings trouble to the nation's institutions. Scandals are likely and government officials may be implicated in them. The government is weak and suffers hindrance. Organized crime becomes more problematic, and intelligence agencies and other secret organizations cause trouble for the government.

THE SUN IN ASPECT

The aspects made by the Sun, in turn, tell you how the head of government relates to the other major powers in the nation. As discussed earlier, each planet corresponds to one of the basic elements of a human society: the Sun to the head of government and more generally to the political system; the Moon to the privileged classes, the part of the population that takes an active role in politics; Mercury to intellectuals and the media; Venus to women and women's issues; Mars to men and men's issues; Jupiter to the corporate sector and corporate culture, and to bureaucracies in general; Saturn to the rural hinterlands and their population and concerns, and to institutions and the legacies of the past; Uranus to the subcultures and countercultures where innovation takes place; and Neptune to mass culture and to those trends that rise from the majority, which, in every society, is shut out of the political process.

These basic elements of a modern society overlap in complex ways and interact in even-more-intricate patterns. Their basic relationships at any given time in a specific nation, however, are shown by the aspects made by their respective luminaries and planets to one another. What if one or more of the planets in a chart make no aspects to anything? That tells you that the element of society indicated by that planet is relatively free from outside influences while the chart is in effect. This happens fairly often, of course. In the case of the Sun, a well-dignified Sun free from aspects very often means that the head of government is basically free to do as he or she wills, while a debilitated Sun free from aspects indicates that the head of government is isolated and has little influence on events.

For practical purposes, as discussed in chapter 1, aspects are divided into helpful and hostile categories (remember that a conjunction with a benefic planet is helpful, and a conjunction with a malefic planet is hostile). Each aspect also has its own subtle character—for instance, squares tend to indicate active conflict while oppositions tend to indicate frozen, static conflict—but like most of the fine details of mundane astrology, these points are best learned by close study of actual charts.

Aspects to the Sun also differ in a crucial way, because conjunction with the Sun—or even being close to such a conjunction—may benefit the sun but is always difficult for the other planet involved. Any planet within 8°30' of the Sun is considered "combust," which is a form of debility that weakens the planet and the house or houses that it rules. In practice, what this usually means is that whatever the planet rules in the chart has been co-opted by the head of government or the government generally, and its influence will be used for the advantage of the Sun's representative rather than for its own ends. If the combust planet is strong otherwise, it may be able to exact some benefit in return. If it is weak, it can count on being exploited and dumped in the usual fashion.

With these considerations kept in mind, the Sun's aspects to the other planets in the chart have these general meanings.

SUN CONJUNCT OR IN HELPFUL ASPECT TO MOON

The head of government and the political classes are in harmony with each other. More generally, harmonious relations among the classes of society, and between the government and the people. This is a very fortunate aspect, indicating prosperity and success.

SUN IN HOSTILE ASPECT TO MOON

The head of government and the political classes are at odds. More generally, conflict among social classes, or between political parties or influential sectors of society. The government is unpopular and faces difficulties. Strikes or discontent on the part of the working classes are likely. This is also an unfortunate aspect for public health, though it does not predict serious problems unless supported by other indications in the chart.

SUN CONJUNCT MERCURY

Mercury never gets far enough from the Sun to form any aspect but the conjunction. This is favorable for intellectual, scientific, and literary activities, which can count on receiving help or honor from the government. Aspects of this kind also predict important speeches and successful public relations on the part of the head of government and the government generally.

SUN IN HOSTILE ASPECT TO MERCURY

Mercury never gets far enough from the Sun to form a hostile aspect. The dependence of Mercury on the Sun is reflected in the dependence of intellectuals on the political system. Only since the discovery of Uranus in 1781 have intellectuals routinely come into conflict with the established political order, and when they do, it is because they belong to a Uranian subculture or counterculture and have left the influence of Mercury.

SUN CONJUNCT VENUS

Venus is the Lesser Benefic, and so a conjunction between her and the Sun is an indication of national prosperity and success. It is fortunate for the government and the nation. The economy benefits, with tourism, entertainment industries, and consumer expenditures generally driving growth. Relations with other countries tend to be friendly and mutually profitable. Aspects of this kind are also favorable for government policy toward the arts and creative activities generally, and for laws affecting women's issues.

SUN IN HOSTILE ASPECT TO VENUS

The only hostile aspect Venus can make with the Sun is the semisquare of 45°, a minor aspect. When this occurs, it tends to be unfortunate for the government and the nation, predicting some degree of political and economic trouble, but it is rarely significant unless it is reinforced by at least one other hostile aspect. This aspect can also warn of troubles for the arts and for the creative sector in general, and for women's issues.

SUN IN HELPFUL ASPECT TO MARS

This is a strong indication of change for the better and especially predicts improvements in public health and in the position of the nation relative to foreign powers. It brings strength and success to the government and is especially fortunate in military affairs. In time of war, it predicts success in battle and, if reinforced by other indications, can bring hostilities to a successful conclusion. Aspects of this kind are also favorable for men's issues.

SUN CONJUNCT OR IN HOSTILE
ASPECT TO MARS

A difficult and sometimes disastrous indication, this warns of conflict and disagreement either internally or with other countries. The house occupied by Mars is the likely focus of the dispute. An aspect of this kind predicts heated public passions and belligerent attitudes toward the perceived enemy, whether internal or external. Partisan hatreds in politics are accentuated, and the government risks becoming the target of opposition and hostile passions on the part of the masses. Violence against government officials is possible. Men's issues lose ground. The military is troubled. In war, unless countered by favorable aspects, this can be an indicator of lost battles and, if strongly placed, of defeat at the hands of rival nations.

SUN CONJUNCT OR IN
HELPFUL ASPECT TO JUPITER

The most favorable aspect in mundane astrology, a helpful aspect between the Sun and the Greater Benefic promises peace and prosperity at home and abroad. The government receives a significant helping of simple good luck. The economy improves, and relations with other countries are friendly.

The corporate sector behaves in ways that benefit the common good. Philanthropy becomes more widespread, and serious social problems can be addressed constructively. Wealth is available for constructive purposes.

SUN IN HOSTILE ASPECT TO JUPITER

Aspects of this kind bring difficulties for trade and commerce, tangled legal cases of national importance, and worsening public health. Its most common keynote, however, is scandal, affecting the government, the privileged classes, the corporate sector, or society in general, depending on other indications. Lurid events and highly publicized crimes seize the public imagination and cause a loss of public confidence in any or all of these.

SUN IN HELPFUL ASPECT TO SATURN

Aspects of this kind give the government strength rather than popularity and enable it to hold or extend its power by skillful maneuvering and prudent management. The rural hinterlands benefit under this aspect, and the working classes generally can expect improved conditions. Aspects of this kind are also fortunate for state and local officials, and reforms on the state and local levels carried out under these aspects will be fortunate.

SUN CONJUNCT OR IN HOSTILE ASPECT TO SATURN

Hostile aspects between the Sun and the Greater Malefic are very difficult indications in a mundane chart. They predict a loss of power and popularity on the part of the government or its head, obstacles and delays confronting the affairs of the nation, or conflict between the head of government and the national legislature or between the two houses of the legislature. The economy stagnates or suffers a downturn, and social life and the activities of the privileged classes are overshadowed by depression or subject to misfortunes. This is also an unfavorable indication for public health and for state and local officials.

SUN IN HELPFUL ASPECT TO URANUS

These aspects promise successful reforms and changes for the better. New ideas enter the public conversation, new and beneficial laws are passed, and the nation is full of new life and energy. Unless other indications in the chart contradict this, this class of aspects predicts success abroad and domestically and brings strength and prosperity to the government and the nation. New creative and cultural ventures are favored.

SUN CONJUNCT OR IN HOSTILE
ASPECT TO URANUS

Another very difficult indication, predicting sudden and unexpected troubles for the government and its head. These aspects often indicate bad decisions and false steps on the part of government. Misguided legislation or policy, unwise or unpopular reforms, a refusal to listen to good advice, and autocratic use of power are common under these aspects. As a result, troubles abound, alliances break down, governments fail to achieve their goals or fall from power, and elections are lost. Strikes and riots are likely when these aspects are in effect.

SUN IN HELPFUL ASPECT TO NEPTUNE

Under these aspects the government is popular with the masses and can count on their support. Success comes through popular enthusiasm or sheer dumb luck. Peace and prosperity are likely. The government encourages people to do what they would do anyway, and benefits as a result. A period of relative calm and contentment in which little of importance happens.

SUN CONJUNCT OR IN HOSTILE
ASPECT TO NEPTUNE

This is far and away the most unfortunate indication in a mundane chart. H. S. Green's classic formulation has not yet been bettered: "Something in the nature of a downfall or collapse takes place." Confusion, disorder, and the failure of legislation or policy can be expected, and lurid scandals come to light. Unpopularity and misfortune are in store for those in power. If other indications support this, the government is at risk of being thrown out of power, either through elections or by some less formal means. Under almost any conditions, the position, reputation, or life of some important political figure is at risk.

* * *

Remember in using the paragraphs above, as well as their equivalents in the chapters to come, that these are general indications and not hard-and-fast rules. Over time, as you study mundane charts and compare them to how events actually turned out, you will develop your own personal sense of what each placement means, and you should let that sense guide you. Since we don't yet know what causes the effects that allow the positions of the heavens to predict events on Earth, astrology in practice is always an art as well as a science, and the intuition that comes from training and experience is a necessary factor in making accurate predictions.

Remember also that a mundane chart, like any other astrological chart, must always be read as a whole. If a mundane chart has a well-dignified Sun in the 7th house, let's say, but the cusp of the 7th is ruled by Saturn and he is in his fall in Aries and afflicted by squares with Mars and Uranus, the good indications of the Sun's placement emphatically do not overrule the negative indications of the house ruler's condition. Equally, though, the Sun's effects are not overruled; the result of a combination like this one would be a generally dismal time for the nation's foreign affairs, as shown by the house ruler, but with one major success in the midst of all the trouble, as shown by the Sun.

CHAPTER 4

THE MOON

In traditional mundane astrology, the Moon has generally been held to represent the people rather than the government and its head, which are indicated by the Sun. In my own experience, I have found that this attribution needs to be taken in a somewhat narrower sense. I find that the Moon represents that fraction of the public that has a voice in a nation's political life. This is always a minority, though it can be a larger or smaller minority depending on the political and social structure of the nation.

We can speak of that minority as the political class of a society. What puts people in or out of the political class varies from nation to nation, culture to culture, and age to age. It can be ethnicity, it can be gender, it can be caste, it can be religion, but in the societies of the modern industrial West, it's normally a matter of social class, and thus of income level. Generally speaking, in a modern industrial society, the sector of the population from the upper middle class on up—say, the upper 20% or so by income, more or less—have access to the political process. Those whose incomes place them below this line do not.

Mundane astrology allows this distinction to be expressed elegantly in charts. The Moon represents the political classes, who claim to speak for the public as a whole, while the first house and its ruler represent the masses, whose opinions may or may not have anything to do with whatever the political classes may be saying. When the Moon is in the first house or in a helpful aspect to the first house's ruler, the interests of the political classes and the general public are aligned with one another. When they are in hostile aspect, their interests are opposed, and when they are out of aspect, what the political classes are saying has little or nothing to do with what the general public is thinking.

The houses the Moon rules or occupies in a mundane chart indicate the department of the national life that will receive particular attention from the political classes during the period for which the chart is cast. The condition of the Moon, in turn, tells you how that department of the national life will affect those members of the public who have a voice in the political process. The aspects the Moon makes with the planetary rulers of each of the houses provide a third level of meaning.

THE MOON IN THE HOUSES

1ST HOUSE

A dignified Moon in or ruling the 1st house indicates that the interests of the political classes and the general public will be closely aligned with one another, and the opinions of the politically active sectors of the public can be treated as a fair reflection of the attitudes of the people as a whole. This placement indicates that the concerns of the people will be prominent in national politics while the chart has effect. It is a sign of general prosperity and contentment and also traditionally predicts good agricultural conditions and an improvement in public health.

A debilitated Moon in or ruling the 1st house also places the interests of the public at center stage, but agitation and turmoil are likely. If the Moon is afflicted by aspect, the houses ruled by the afflicting planet or planets will indicate the source of the unrest. If the Moon is afflicted by her placement in a hostile sign, long-standing popular grievances from a variety of sources are likely to come to a head.

2ND HOUSE

A dignified Moon in or ruling the 2nd house is a very favorable sign in economic matters, predicting general prosperity. It benefits domestic trade and industry, brings improvement in the whole range of financial markets, and increases business profits. While this placement is in effect, new industries and sources of wealth are likely to arise. This is also a favorable placement for agriculture and brings improved tax revenues to national, regional, and local governments.

A debilitated Moon in or ruling the 2nd house is still somewhat favorable, since the Moon is always strong here, but there will be troubles and losses at least partially offsetting the gains noted above. Changes in economic conditions benefit some but impose burdens on others.

3RD HOUSE

A dignified Moon in or ruling the 3rd house is fortunate for the transportation, communication, media, and internet industries. All these can expect increased traffic and improved profits. It is also favorable for the public schools and for the post office. Important issues relating to one or more of these sectors of the economy and society will come in for public discussion.

A debilitated Moon in or ruling the 3rd house brings trouble to transport, communication, media, and the internet. Changes made in these sectors, or in the post office or the public schools, will turn out badly. Traffic and train accidents are more common and costly. False or misleading rumors spread through the political classes.

4TH HOUSE

A dignified Moon in or ruling the 4th house is favorable for agriculture and all resource industries, and also for the rural hinterlands of the nation. It supports the interests of the people against those of the government. This placement is also fortunate for the party out of power in national politics and brings more of the political class into alignment with the opposition party and its causes.

A debilitated Moon in or ruling the 4th house is still somewhat favorable for agriculture and resource industries, since the Moon is always strong in this house, but any gains in these sectors will be balanced by losses elsewhere. Popular discontent in the rural hinterlands becomes a significant political force. Controversies relating to the affairs of this house become prominent. The party out of power will likely be troubled by internal conflicts.

5TH HOUSE

A dignified Moon in or ruling the 5th house is favorable for the entertainment and tourism industries, which can expect improved financial conditions, and speculative markets can expect price increases. General prosperity and contentment are likely when this position is present. The arts and literature flourish. This placement is also favorable for the upper house of the national legislature, which takes a leading role in the political sphere.

A debilitated Moon in or ruling the 5th house predicts difficult times for the entertainment and tourism industry and a downturn in speculative markets. The wealthy end of society is troubled and dissatisfaction is widespread. The upper house of the national legislature is also troubled and will be unable to exercise its functions smoothly, or possibly at all.

6TH HOUSE

A dignified Moon in or ruling the 6th house is favorable for the laboring classes; employment increases and wages and conditions improve, and food and other necessities become more affordable. It also predicts better conditions for the armed forces, which receive ample support, and it is a good sign for public health.

A debilitated Moon in or ruling the 6th house is a warning of trouble in all these sectors of society. The laboring classes are restless and dissatisfied, employment decreases, and wages and benefits suffer. The armed forces are troubled. Food and other necessities suffer price increases or actual shortages. Public health suffers; if the Moon is seriously afflicted when she is in this placement, an epidemic is likely.

7TH HOUSE

A dignified Moon in or ruling the 7th house is favorable for foreign policy and amicable relations with other countries. It is an indication of peace rather than war. It also predicts a constructive relationship between the political classes and the public in general, bringing public concerns to the fore and favoring the settlement of social problems.

A debilitated Moon in or ruling the 7th house heralds trouble in foreign affairs and hostile relations with other countries. If the Moon in this placement is afflicted by a hostile aspect with a malefic planet, there is a serious risk of war. Discontent among the general public is likely, and issues relating to the people are a source of significant trouble.

8TH HOUSE

A dignified Moon in or ruling the 8th house is favorable for foreign trade and investment. The balance of trade improves, and funds from abroad flow into the markets. The Moon is naturally weak in this house, however, and an increase in the death rate through disease or other causes can be expected.

A debilitated Moon in or ruling the 8th house foretells trouble with foreign trade and investment. Funds flow out of domestic markets in search of higher yields elsewhere. The balance of trade worsens. The death rate increases; if the Moon is seriously afflicted when she is in this placement, an epidemic is likely.

9TH HOUSE

A dignified Moon in or ruling the 9th house is favorable for religion, higher education, and all things at a distance. Tourism benefits from this placement, and it is favorable for airlines and shipping. Rulings from the nation's highest court are popular among the political classes. Astrologers also benefit from this placement.

A debilitated Moon in or ruling the 9th house is a sign of trouble for airlines and shipping companies. Tourism falls off and the universities suffer. Religious movements become a source of trouble, either by causing public unrest or through highly publicized scandals. Decisions of the highest court are unpopular among the political classes, and efforts may be made to restrict judicial independence. Astrologers suffer from this placement.

10TH HOUSE

A dignified Moon in or ruling the 10th house makes the government or its leader popular with the political classes. The Moon is weak in this house, and so the political classes very often lose some of their capacity for independent thought and action when this placement is in effect, becoming more subservient to the government. Popular issues come to the fore, and public ceremonies of great symbolic importance take place. This placement is also fortunate for trade and the national economy.

A debilitated Moon in or ruling the 10th house is a sign of trouble and discontent throughout the nation. The government may be passive in the face of serious issues or may make bad decisions in dealing with the nation's problems. The political class and the government are at odds, issues of concern to the people are neglected, and the country is restless and sullen. Trade and the national economy suffer.

11TH HOUSE

A dignified Moon in or ruling the 11th house is favorable for the national legislature and especially the lower house, which will show more vigor and more responsiveness to public needs than usual. The executive and legislative branches work in harmony together. Important legislation is passed. The government receives general support from the political class.

A debilitated Moon in or ruling the 11th house predicts trouble for the government. Legislation and policy measures prove to be unfortunate, conflict emerges within and between the parties, and the party in power loses ground. Legislation is delayed or blocked altogether. The nation loses friends abroad.

12TH HOUSE

A dignified Moon in or ruling the 12th house is favorable for national institutions, which receive the respect and patronage of the political classes. Institutions receive public support and undergo needed reforms. Charitable projects thrive.

A debilitated Moon in or ruling the 12th house brings trouble for the nation's institutions and causes charitable projects to struggle. The crime rate increases. Institutions face hostile criticism or a simple lack of interest from the public, and scandals are likely in the institutional sector. The nation is at risk due to the activities of secret enemies.

THE MOON IN ASPECT

The distinction between the Moon and whatever planet rules the 1st house, the house of the population in general, is crucial to understand the aspects the Moon makes with the other planets in the chart. The placement and condition of the Moon tell you how the political class will fare during the period ruled by whatever mundane chart you're considering. The aspects made by the Moon, in turn, will show you how the political class interacts with the other principal factors in national life. The fate and interactions of the bulk of the population are shown instead by the planet ruling the 1st house.

The aspects the Moon makes to other planets take their meaning in turn from the twofold signification of each planet. On the one hand, as discussed in an earlier chapter, each planet has its own meaning in terms of the basic factors in human society: thus, Mercury relates to the intellectual class and people in the communications media, Venus to women, Mars to men, and so on. On the other hand, the sign on the cusp of each house tells you which planet rules that house, and thus the affairs of that house. If the cusp of the 2nd house is in Gemini, for example, Mercury's influence is not limited to the intellectual class; while the chart in question has effect, Mercury also rules the nation's economic life, and an aspect between the Moon and Mercury will tell you how the political class relates to economic conditions while the chart is in effect. The placement and condition of Mercury in that case, in turn, also indicates what general economic conditions will be like during the same period, and aspects the Moon makes to Mercury will have the same twofold significance. Be sure to read the aspects in both senses as you sort out the meanings of the chart.

Among the most-important things to watch in terms of lunar aspects with house rulers is any aspect between the Moon and the ruler of the 1st house. The long-term stability and survival of any nation depends on the willingness of the political class to act for the good of the entire population, rather than pursuing its own advantage at the expense of everyone else. Favorable aspects between the Moon and the 1st-house ruler thus generally benefit the nation as a whole. A prolonged series of hostile aspects between the Moon and the ruler of the 1st house very often means that the political class has lost track of the basic realities of governance, and turmoil can be expected to follow in relatively short order.

With this in mind, let's go through the aspects made by the Moon with other planets (aspects between the Sun and Moon were covered in the previous chapter and will not be repeated here). The Moon's aspects have the following general meanings:

MOON CONJUNCT OR IN HELPFUL ASPECT WITH MERCURY

Scientific, educational, and intellectual concerns receive more support from the political class. New discoveries in science and technology are publicized. This is a favorable indication for treaties and improvements in communications and travel between nations, and it also favors the introduction or passage of important legislation. Speeches, essays, or internet posts will have more influence than usual on public opinion, and, if Mercury is strong, they may cause sudden shifts in the political or cultural climate.

MOON IN HOSTILE ASPECT WITH MERCURY

Controversies and disputes can be expected, especially but not only over scientific, educational, and intellectual concerns. Claims made concerning new scientific and technological discoveries will turn out to be inaccurate or fraudulent. Disagreements between nations break out, and diplomatic relations will be troubled. Slander, libel, forgery, and fraud will be more common than usual and, if other indications support this, may cause serious trouble in the political, economic, or cultural spheres. Legislation is delayed or fails.

MOON CONJUNCT OR IN HELPFUL ASPECT WITH VENUS

A favorable indication for prosperity, especially influencing agriculture and the tourism and entertainment industries. The public mood is upbeat, money moves into productive investments, and charitable projects flourish. Issues of importance to women receive useful attention. This is a favorable condition for foreign relations and is especially so for meetings of heads of state and for international events of all kinds. Nations in trouble will receive ample and timely assistance.

MOON IN HOSTILE ASPECT WITH VENUS

This is unfavorable for the economy, predicting excessive government expenditures and volatility in stocks and other speculative markets. An important firm faces bankruptcy. Women's issues are ignored or burdened with unhelpful laws and regulations. Financial relations with other countries are troubled, and trade policy becomes a subject of dispute within and between nations. The tourism and entertainment industries face difficult times, and the agricultural sector is troubled.

MOON IN HELPFUL ASPECT WITH MARS

This strengthens the nation and brings energy and activity into its affairs abroad and at home. The military receives support from the political class. In time of peace, defenses are strengthened, the nation's military situation improves vis-à-vis its rivals abroad, and peace is likely to be preserved. Issues important to men receive constructive attention. If a war is already in process when this condition comes into effect, success can be expected and forces can be sent abroad with good prospects of victory.

MOON CONJUNCT OR IN HOSTILE ASPECT WITH MARS

An indication of trouble, disputation, and violence. If either planet is in an angular house or close to one of the four angles, war is a serious possibility. Otherwise, disputes with other countries cannot be resolved easily, or at all. A warlike mood grips the country, making compromise difficult and fostering extreme opinions and actions. Riots and civil unrest are likely, as are deaths and disasters relating to the military. Issues of importance to men are ignored or suffer setbacks.

MOON CONJUNCT OR IN HELPFUL ASPECT WITH JUPITER

A very favorable sign, predicting peace and prosperity. The economy expands, trade and manufacture are prosperous, and agriculture is fortunate. Charitable projects thrive. This is especially fortunate for foreign trade, and also for air travel and ventures into outer space. The public mood is calm, expansive, and generous.

MOON IN HOSTILE ASPECT WITH JUPITER

Any lunar aspect with Jupiter, even a hostile one, tends to bring prosperity and peace, but a hostile aspect between these planets also warns of extravagance and waste through excessive public expenditures or the excesses of the rich. Scandals are likely and, if either planet is angular, may end the career of an influential political or cultural figure. Public health declines due to overindulgence of various kinds and its results.

MOON IN HELPFUL ASPECT WITH SATURN

A favorable aspect for domestic calm and stability. Obstacles to the smooth functioning of public affairs are removed, and the political class tends to win the goodwill of the population as a whole through constructive action. The economy improves through increased efficiency and the elimination of extravagance and waste. Employment opportunities increase. Savings and productive investments prosper and speculation is curbed. Reforms dealing with the activities of local and regional governments are likely.

MOON CONJUNCT OR IN HOSTILE
ASPECT WITH SATURN

This very difficult indication warns of misfortune to the political class and the country. The political class and the masses are at odds. The political system fails to work smoothly and may not function at all. The economy is depressed and disordered, trade suffers, unemployment rises, and markets sink. This aspect can indicate the death of an influential political figure. One difficulty is followed by another, and nothing goes right for the government, the political classes, or society as a whole. If Saturn is angular and other indications support this, the collapse of a government may follow.

MOON IN HELPFUL ASPECT WITH URANUS

Fortunate for the political classes and the legislative branch of government, this fosters beneficial changes and reforms. Popular support and approval for the country's leadership are likely. Energy and enthusiasm are abundant in the nation's life. New social movements, innovative technologies, and ideas for the future attract attention and followers.

MOON CONJUNCT OR IN HOSTILE
ASPECT WITH URANUS

Disorder, confusion, and delay beset the political class, the government, and society as a whole. The government's policies are unpopular, and the government itself is the focus of public anger and hostility. New laws enacted and policies put into place during this aspect will fail to achieve their ends and will arouse opposition. If other indications support this, the government may fall or be forced to retract its policy positions.

MOON IN HELPFUL ASPECT WITH NEPTUNE

The political class is more than usually attentive to the needs of the general population and wins support from the people as a result. Popular movements thrive and win support for their goals. This is a good indication for prosperity and contentment for the nation and tends also to suggest a state of peace with other nations.

MOON CONJUNCT OR IN HOSTILE ASPECT WITH NEPTUNE

The political class fails to listen to the concerns of the general population, which responds with resentment and hostility. Class conflict increases. Public scandals are likely and lurid crimes come to light. False rumors and dubious claims spread rapidly through society, heightening the tension. Trust in authorities and in the system of government is weakened. If Neptune is angular and other indications support this, the government may fall due to its inability to maintain the support of the people.

CHAPTER 5

MERCURY

In traditional mundane astrology, Mercury represents the mental dimension of a nation, from its highest to its lowest expressions. It stands for the nation's intellectuals and creative minds, but also for its talking heads, media figures, and vendors of ready-made opinions, and for the chattering classes who set the overall tone of the collective conversation of the time. It stands for laws and regulations, treaties, and all agreements within and between nations.

Mercury in mundane charts also represents every form of communication and transportation, as well as the news media and, in modern times, the internet. When it is strongly placed or dignified by good aspects, expect ideas to play a more important role than usual in the national life. When it is weakly placed or afflicted by bad aspects, the ideas that take center stage are more likely to be dysfunctional or confused, and communication and transportation technologies may suffer breakdowns.

The houses that Mercury rules or occupies in a mundane chart indicate the department of the national life that will be important in the collective conversation of the nation during the period for which the chart is cast. The condition of Mercury in that house, in turn, tells you how that department of the national life will affect the media and the communication and transportation industries. The aspects that Mercury makes with the planetary rulers of each of the houses provide a third level of meaning, which we'll get to later in this chapter.

MERCURY IN THE HOUSES

1ST HOUSE

A dignified Mercury in or ruling the 1st house encourages public discussion and makes the ideas and interests of the common people more prominent than usual in the collective conversation of the time. Speechmaking, public meetings, publications, and discussions on the media or on internet forums will play a larger-than-usual role in setting the tone of public discourse. Literature, education, and science benefit. This placement also tends to improve traditions for trade and is thus favorable for the economy.

A debilitated Mercury in or ruling the 1st house stirs up public disagreements and political controversies. Speeches, publications, and other forms of communication have unexpected and disruptive results. Libels and slanders are common and can cause a public furor. Literature, education, and science suffer. This placement also yields discouraging conditions for trade and leads to economic weakness.

2ND HOUSE

A dignified Mercury in or ruling the 2nd house is very favorable for industries that have to do with communications, transportation, media, and the internet. More generally, it enhances trade and brings improved tax revenue to the government. Literature, education, and science prosper. Changes in the laws or regulations governing transportation or other Mercurial subjects are beneficial under this aspect.

A debilitated Mercury in or ruling the 2nd house foretells a downturn for industries that relate to communications, transportation, media, and the internet. Trade is weak and government revenues decrease. Volatility in the stock market is likely, and rumors and false reports concerning stocks are rife. Frauds, thefts, and forgeries are common. Avoid speculative investments at this time.

3RD HOUSE

A dignified Mercury in or ruling the 3rd house encourages useful innovation in communications, transportation, and education. It fosters new enterprises in these fields and leads to change in familiar patterns of activity and traffic. Under this placement, advertising campaigns tend to be more successful, and governments are more likely to listen to their constituencies and take constructive action as a result.

A debilitated Mercury in or ruling the 3rd house is the classic sign of failed innovation. New technologies introduced or promoted during this time will not live up to their promise, and businesses in these fields founded under this placement tend to fail. It is especially unfavorable for education. Expect an unusually high number of accidents in transport while this is in effect. Advertising campaigns will be unsuccessful, and governments will neither listen to their constituencies nor communicate effectively with them.

4TH HOUSE

A dignified Mercury in or ruling the 4th house is favorable for infrastructure improvement and repair; bridges are rebuilt, roads are resurfaced, phone and internet service are improved, and other projects related to communication and transportation tend to receive useful attention. Major public works are likely under this placement. The party out of power is more likely to reach out successfully to voters. The concerns of the rural hinterlands of the nation are more likely to be heard and addressed. This placement is also favorable for employment, and for the prosperity of rural areas and small towns.

A debilitated Mercury in or ruling the 4th house warns of trouble for the nation's infrastructure; depending on the nature of the debility, it may be neglected, or "improvements" put in place may make matters worse. The party out of power fails to listen to the concerns of voters. The concerns of the rural hinterlands suffer from even more neglect than usual. Unemployment and discontent tend to be more widespread under this placement, and the crops suffer.

5TH HOUSE

A dignified Mercury in or ruling the 5th house is very fortunate for speculative markets of all kinds, though volatility is also likely—Mercury is never a stabilizing influence! It benefits the entertainment and tourism industries, which have an easier time attracting customers. Under this placement the arts and culture generally tend to prosper. The upper house of the national legislature becomes more active than usual and may take the lead in lawmaking.

A debilitated Mercury in or ruling the 5th house is a bad sign for speculative markets of all kinds, warning of volatility with plenty of room to the downside. Frauds and swindles in speculative markets are more likely than usual. The entertainment and tourism industries suffer, as do the arts and culture generally. The upper house of the national legislature is more than usually detached from the concerns of the public and is unlikely to accomplish anything of importance while this placement is in effect.

6TH HOUSE

A dignified Mercury in or ruling the 6th house is a beneficial sign for the laboring classes, which prosper under this placement. Unemployment decreases, laws and regulations governing workplaces are improved, and the collective conversation of the time is more likely to take the needs of the working classes into account. This placement is also favorable for public health and can announce the arrival of improvements in healthcare. Under this placement the military benefits from new technology and improved communications.

A debilitated Mercury in or ruling the 6th house announces hard times for the laboring classes. Unemployment rises, and laws and regulations governing workplaces either are not enforced or become burdensome rather than helpful. The concerns of the working classes are excluded from the collective conversation of the time. Public health worsens; if Mercury in this placement is afflicted by Mars, Saturn, Uranus, or the ruler of the 8th house, an epidemic is likely. The military is unfortunate and has trouble finding adequate recruits.

7TH HOUSE

A dignified Mercury in or ruling the 7th house brings public discussion of foreign affairs. New treaties, trade agreements, and legislation affecting relations with other countries are proposed or enacted. Official visits and summit meetings with foreign officials are common under this placement. Much diplomatic activity takes place, though this may not become public. This placement is favorable for peace, though it may not be durable.

A debilitated Mercury in or ruling the 7th house portends trouble over foreign affairs. Public debate and dissension over foreign relations are likely. Treaty negotiations fail or produce an unsatisfactory result. Communication among nations is hindered or interrupted; ambassadors may be withdrawn and friendly relations broken off. If other indications concur, disputes between nations risk spiraling out of control, and war is possible.

8TH HOUSE

A dignified Mercury in or ruling the 8th house is favorable for foreign trade and investment. Trade agreements and regulations proposed or enacted under this placement will be beneficial. The country prospers through its economic relations with other countries.

A debilitated Mercury in or ruling the 8th house brings trouble for foreign trade and investment. Trade agreements and regulations proposed or enacted under this placement will fail or will yield unwelcome results. Since this is also the house of death, if Mercury in this placement is afflicted by Mars, Saturn, Uranus, or the lord of the 6th house, a serious epidemic is likely.

9TH HOUSE

A dignified Mercury in or ruling the 9th house is favorable for higher education, air travel, and scientific discovery, especially when this involves great distance in space or time—for example, space travel is fortunate under this influence. Court cases dealing with communication, transportation, intellectual property, and other Mercurial matters benefit the nation. Religious organizations benefit, as does astrology.

A debilitated Mercury in or ruling the 9th house is unfavorable for higher education, air travel, and science. Aircraft crashes are more likely, and long-distance travel is disrupted. The law courts are unusually busy, and rulings are likely to be unfortunate for the nation.

10TH HOUSE

A dignified Mercury in or ruling the 10th house brings good fortune to the government through effective communication and accurate information. Government policies are intelligently drafted and carried through successfully. All Mercurial matters prosper from this placement. It also announces important public ceremonies, speechmaking, and significant political events.

A debilitated Mercury in or ruling the 10th house brings trouble on the government through bad communication and inaccurate information. The government will be out of touch with the interests and concerns of the people, and its laws, policies, and pronouncements will be ignored or criticized. Public agitation and debate over politics is heightened. Trade and all Mercurial matters suffer under this placement.

11TH HOUSE

A dignified Mercury in or ruling the 11th house is favorable for the activities of the national legislature, especially the lower house. Legislation progresses, and debates in the legislature are productive and lead to improved laws. Laws and policies affecting the legislature change in helpful ways. Trade, transport, communication, and the media receive constructive attention from the legislature.

A debilitated Mercury in or ruling the 11th house is unfavorable for the legislature and predicts debate, dissension, and division. Legislation is stalled or turns out to have unfortunate effects. Public disaffection with the laws or the legislative branch increases. Disputes between the branches of government or between the parties are bitter and unproductive.

12TH HOUSE

A dignified Mercury in or ruling the 12th house brings substantial benefits to the nation's institutions, which are subject to public discussion and constructive change. Prison reform is likely. Intelligence agencies are able to gather accurate information, and their reports to government are more likely to lead to constructive policy. New organizations and movements for positive change are likely to arise.

A debilitated Mercury in or ruling the 12th house warns of corruption, dishonesty, and incompetence in the nation's institutions. Fraud and forgery are brought to light, and the reputation of the institutional sector suffers. The nation may be at risk from secret activities among its enemies, foreign and domestic, with espionage especially likely. Not all those who claim to be friendly to the nation should be trusted.

MERCURY IN ASPECT

Aspects between Mercury and the Sun or Moon are covered in earlier chapters.

MERCURY CONJUNCT OR IN HELPFUL
ASPECT WITH VENUS

A mildly favorable aspect for national peace, contentment, and goodwill, this signals the fading out of old grievances and sources of discontent and the rise of general tranquility. If supported by other indications, it is beneficial for prosperity and national finances and indicates an economic climate favoring new business enterprises and decreased unemployment. It is also a favorable indication for women's issues.

MERCURY IN HOSTILE
ASPECT WITH VENUS

A mildly unfavorable aspect for the national mood. Existing grievances and sources of discontent can be expected to remain significant, or new causes of dissatisfaction found. If supported by other indications, it warns of troubled economic conditions and increased unemployment. It is also an unfavorable indication for women's issues.

MERCURY IN HELPFUL
ASPECT WITH MARS

A favorable sign for all Mercurial affairs, giving additional energy and activity throughout the intellectual sphere and the communication and transportation industries. If Mercury is well dignified, technological innovations are favored and will likely be profitable. Education, literary activities, and the sciences flourish. It also brings attention to men's issues.

MERCURY CONJUNCT OR IN HOSTILE
ASPECT WITH MARS

This aspect turns public discussions angry and hostile, generates ill feeling between different sectors of society, and generates high feeling and public acrimony. Legal and political disputes flare up. Strikes, protests, and riots are more prominent than usual. The crime rate increases, and public outrage toward criminal activity becomes vocal. This aspect is also unfortunate for men's issues.

MERCURY CONJUNCT OR IN HELPFUL
ASPECT WITH JUPITER

Favorable for peace, contentment, and prosperity, this aspect indicates an expansion of trade and commerce. It is very favorable for education, literary activities, and the sciences, all of which can receive increased funding and popular support. If supported by other indications, this aspect is favorable for new legislation.

MERCURY IN HOSTILE ASPECT WITH JUPITER

Unfortunate for the communication and transport sectors of the economy, which must cope with unexpected difficulties. Education faces setbacks and may be called to account for its handling of money. Frauds and swindles are more common than usual. Beware of rising prices in stock markets or other investment venues while this aspect is in effect, since there is likely to be deception involved, and prices may drop even faster than they rose.

MERCURY IN HELPFUL ASPECT WITH SATURN

A very favorable aspect for transport and communication infrastructure: new projects along these lines set in motion under this aspect will provide lasting benefit, and investments of this kind will prosper. Favorable for new regulations, and improvements and upgrades of all kinds. This aspect also favors the laboring classes and brings higher wages and improved work conditions; unemployment decreases and the economy benefits as a result.

MERCURY CONJUNCT OR IN HOSTILE
ASPECT WITH SATURN

This difficult aspect brings trouble to the communications and transport sector and to society in general. Trade and commerce are hindered, transportation is delayed, conditions worsen for the laboring classes, and strikes, protests, and disturbances are likely. Education, literary activities, and the sciences all suffer. Infrastructure projects and legislation set in motion under this aspect will bog down or fail to accomplish their goals.

MERCURY IN HELPFUL ASPECT WITH URANUS

Beneficial for the political sphere, this aspect encourages reform, and legislation proposed, debated, or enacted while it is in effect is more likely to be successful and popular. Changes for the better can be expected. Scientific discovery and technological innovation, especially but not only in the communication and transport sectors, benefit from this aspect. Literary and educational matters benefit from innovation as well. Public enthusiasm for change is high, and political meetings and debates are well attended.

MERCURY CONJUNCT OR IN HOSTILE ASPECT WITH URANUS

An aspect of political turbulence. Political activity is high, debates and meetings generate high feelings in the public, but delays, difficulties, crises, and complications arise. Unexpected troubles are likely. Strange events and unsolved crimes become subjects of obsessive public interest. If other indications support this, public excitement can turn to anger, resulting in protests, riots, and political crimes.

MERCURY IN HELPFUL ASPECT WITH NEPTUNE

This aspect is favorable for the collective imagination and favors new ideas, aspirations, and efforts in the arts, literature, and culture. If other indications support this, it can inspire new political or social movements or give new vitality and inspiration to existing movements. It favors the emergence of new fads and fashions.

MERCURY CONJUNCT OR IN HOSTILE ASPECT WITH NEPTUNE

A harbinger of remarkable frauds and manias, this aspect leads the collective imagination in strange and unhealthful directions. It can inspire speculative bubbles, apocalyptic frenzies, and other delusional mass movements, and if other indications support this, these can result in a great deal of disruption and chaos. Lurid crimes, real or imagined, seize the public imagination.

CHAPTER 6

VENUS

In traditional mundane astrology, Venus is a benefic planet and indicates good fortune in general. It also represents the women of the nation for which the chart is cast. Modern mundane astrologers such as Raphael and H. S. Green extended that to women's issues and the laws governing women, which had become significant political and social factors in their time, and the same logic deserves to be extended further now that women have become fully empowered political individuals in all Western nations and many countries outside the West. We can therefore read Venus as an indicator of the women's vote, of issues and stances supported principally by women, and of everything else that concerns women collectively in national life.

Venus is also traditionally associated with arts, music, literature, and culture, and these correspondences should also be kept in mind while interpreting charts, especially when house placement supports a meaning of this kind.

The houses that Venus rules or occupies in a mundane chart indicate the department of the national life that will be of particular concern to women during the period for which the chart is cast. The condition of Venus, in turn, tells you how that department of the national life will affect the women of the nation.

Alongside the considerations just mentioned, Venus's placements and rulerships in the charts have the following general meanings:

VENUS IN THE HOUSES

1ST HOUSE

A dignified Venus in or ruling the 1st house is favorable for all issues of concern to women and brings issues of this kind to the center of public interest and discussion. It signals a time of peace, prosperity, and contentment in the nation and is especially favorable for tourism and the entertainment industries.

A debilitated Venus in or ruling the 1st house reverses most of these indications, warning of controversies in society and bad feeling among different social classes. It indicates that women's concerns will be neglected or actively harmed. Public scandals are likely under this influence.

2ND HOUSE

A dignified Venus in or ruling the 2nd house is a very fortunate sign for the nation's economic life, promising general prosperity and improved conditions for business and benefiting the government through increased tax revenues. It also benefits the arts and all forms of culture, as well as businesses catering to amusements, entertainment, and festivities.

A debilitated Venus in or ruling the 2nd house brings extravagant government expenditure, corruption, and waste. Violent fluctuations in the stock market are likely, and speculation will tend to take the place of constructive investment, weakening the economy in the longer term. Dishonesty, embezzlement, and financial scandal can be expected.

3RD HOUSE

A dignified Venus in or ruling the 3rd house is fortunate for the entire economic sector ruled by this house. Transportation, communication, media, and internet businesses will prosper, and travel and tourism also benefit. This placement can also indicate benefits to literacy and to the education of children. In conjunction with other factors, it predicts friendly relations with neighboring countries.

A debilitated Venus in or ruling the 3rd house brings bad news for industries ruled by this house. Waste, extravagance, and poor decisions by businesses in this sector are likely; it is an unfortunate time to launch any new venture in these fields, since public opinion will not favor it. Trouble can be expected for the schools, and relations with neighboring countries will be fraught with potential for conflict and misunderstanding.

4TH HOUSE

A dignified Venus in or ruling the 4th house is a very good indication for agriculture, promising prosperity for farm country and, if present in a chart ruling the autumn, a profitable harvest. It also favors the interests of the rural hinterland generally. Since this house rules the party out of power, it suggests that this party will have success in appealing to the women's vote or in addressing women's issues. It predicts increased involvement by women in the grassroots level of politics.

A debilitated Venus in or ruling the 4th house brings bad weather and troubled times for the agricultural sector and the rural hinterlands. If it appears in a chart that rules the autumn, the harvest will be unprofitable. It predicts trouble for the party out of power, which does not appeal to women in the electorate or fails to address issues of concern to women. It is also unfavorable for the involvement of women in the political process.

5TH HOUSE

A dignified Venus in or ruling the 5th house is a very favorable omen for the whole range of entertainment industries and is especially favorable for the stage and the cinema. It predicts good times and rising prices in speculative markets and benefits celebrities and the well-to-do; it is the best possible time for a female celebrity-to-be to make her public debut. Since the 5th also governs the upper house of the legislature, this placement brings good fortune to the upper house and fosters collegiality and cooperation across party lines.

A debilitated Venus in or ruling the 5th house brings bad business decisions, extravagance, and scandal to the entertainment industries and lands celebrities in legal trouble of various kinds. It warns of volatility in speculative markets and a risk of serious losses. Investment vehicles during a period ruled by this placement usually promise far more than they deliver, and fraud is rife. The upper house of the legislature is unfortunate and may be a subject of public scandal.

6TH HOUSE

A dignified Venus in or ruling the 6th house predicts improved conditions for the laboring classes, especially but not only in industries that preferentially employ women. It encourages the peaceful settlement of labor disputes and a state of contentment on the part of workers. It is an indication of peace more generally, since the 6th house rules armies and navies, and it also promises improved public health in general as well as for women more particularly.

A debilitated Venus in or ruling the 6th house brings increased unemployment and troubled times for the laboring classes, especially though not only for women in the workforce. Labor disputes will be resolved in ways that penalize workers. Public health worsens, with an increase in sexually transmitted diseases especially likely. Military expenditures will be high but ineffectual; new weapons systems contracted or delivered while this aspect is in effect will fail to perform as desired.

7TH HOUSE

A dignified Venus in or ruling the 7th house is an excellent indication in foreign affairs, promising peace, the amicable resolution of differences, and new agreements and treaties between nations. This placement is often associated with summit meetings or official visits by one country's leadership to another. It can also indicate that the nation acts to improve the condition of women in other countries. If the nation is at war, this placement often indicates that a negotiated peace is likely.

A debilitated Venus in or ruling the 7th house brings trouble and anxiety in foreign affairs and can warn of international scandals. It can predict unwise or unsuccessful agreements between nations. If the nation is at war, attempts at a negotiated peace may seem promising, but they are unlikely to go anywhere.

8TH HOUSE

A dignified Venus in or ruling the 8th house brings improved financial relations with other countries. Foreign trade and investment increase, leading to improved prosperity. This aspect can signal successful trade negotiations between nations.

A debilitated Venus in or ruling the 8th house brings trouble through financial relations with other countries. Foreign trade and investment falter or take on a predatory dimension, weakening the nation economically in order to bring profit to the foreign partner. International scandals and financial crimes are likely. If other indications support this, a famous or influential woman will die.

9TH HOUSE

A dignified Venus in or ruling the 9th house is fortunate for religion, higher education, the legal sphere, and the sciences and improves the condition of women in these fields. The nation's high court can be expected to make fair and constructive decisions affecting women's issues. When it appears along with similar indications, this aspect supports friendly relations with foreign countries and makes war and international conflict less likely.

A debilitated Venus in or ruling the 9th house brings trouble to religious and educational institutions and to the legal and scientific world and weakens the position of women in all these fields. Decisions handed down by the nation's high court affecting women's issues will be unfair or unpopular. It can indicate trouble with foreign affairs.

10TH HOUSE

A dignified Venus in or ruling the 10th house is fortunate for the government and its current head, indicating that the party in power will succeed in appealing to women voters or in addressing women's issues constructively. It is an indication of peace, prosperity, and contentment. It often indicates that public ceremonies or important festivities will be held, and also brings public recognition to artists, writers, performers, and other cultural figures.

A debilitated Venus in or ruling the 10th house warns of scandal in high places—financial, sexual, or both at once, affecting the political establishment. Financial questions relating to influential persons may become a matter of public dispute.

11TH HOUSE

A dignified Venus in or ruling the 11th house is very favorable for the national legislature, and especially for its lower house. A cooperative spirit helps bridge party differences; legislation on financial matters or women's issues proceeds smoothly and has beneficial results. Together with other indications, this predicts that the country will receive support from allies abroad.

A debilitated Venus in or ruling the 11th house predicts trouble for the national legislature, and especially for its lower house. The parties may be united in their pursuit of bad policies based on shared misunderstandings, or corrupt practices may influence all sides equally, with negative impacts on the nation's prosperity and well-being. Scandal affecting individual legislators or the legislature generally is likely.

12TH HOUSE

A dignified Venus in or ruling the 12th house brings success and prosperity to the institutions of national life. Benevolence and charity increase. Secret arrangements with other countries are of benefit, and espionage and other covert activities benefit the nation.

A debilitated Venus in or ruling the 12th house afflicts the institutions of national life with fraud, extravagance, or scandal. Financial questions relating to institutions turn out to be troublesome and may uncover dubious dealings or outright corruption. Secret arrangements with other countries turn out to be more trouble than they are worth, and espionage and other covert activities are a source of trouble and scandal to the nation.

VENUS IN ASPECT

Aspects between Venus and the Sun, Moon, and Mercury are covered in previous chapters.

VENUS IN HELPFUL ASPECT WITH MARS

A favorable aspect for economic matters, this improves business and money matters and shows an improvement of domestic and foreign trade. It also predicts an increase in the birthrate and improved conditions for families. It is fortunate for the entertainment industry.

VENUS CONJUNCT OR IN HOSTILE ASPECT WITH MARS

This is unfortunate for economic conditions, warning of excessive government expenditure and of public and private extravagance. Scandals cause trouble in society. The birthrate declines.

VENUS CONJUNCT OR IN HELPFUL ASPECT WITH JUPITER

One of the best aspects in any mundane chart, the conjunction or benefic aspect of the two benefic planets predicts peace and goodwill domestically and abroad and indicates prosperity and the settlement of quarrels. It is particularly beneficial for the interests of women and for all economic sectors related to Venus.

VENUS IN HOSTILE ASPECT WITH JUPITER

Another difficult indication for economic affairs, this also predicts excessive government expenditures and public and private extravagance. Taxes become a greater economic burden, and the economy suffers accordingly. Fraud, scandal, and excessive luxury are widespread, and the nation is troubled as a result.

VENUS IN HELPFUL ASPECT WITH SATURN

Saturn is often a difficult planet in mundane charts, but a helpful aspect from a benefic planet makes him a much more favorable indicator. This aspect predicts good economic news, general improvements in prosperity, increases in stock prices, and improvements in government revenue as a result of increased national wealth. It indicates modest but steady and enduring gains.

VENUS CONJUNCT OR IN HOSTILE
ASPECT WITH SATURN

This aspect, on the other hand, is very bad news indeed. It warns of hard times for industry and the economy generally, losses in the stock markets, and trouble in the banking industry in particular. Social and family life are adversely affected, and poverty becomes more widespread. Women's issues suffer.

VENUS IN HELPFUL ASPECT WITH URANUS

Generally fortunate for prosperity and progress, this aspect is an indication of new legislation or regulations that benefit the economy and the status of households. It is also especially favorable for women's issues, indicating beneficial changes in the laws. It can also indicate a significant positive change in foreign policy.

VENUS CONJUNCT OR IN HOSTILE
ASPECT WITH URANUS

Unfortunate for the economy, this aspect also brings widespread dissatisfaction and dissent with the existing order of society. Family, community, and social troubles become more widespread, and women's issues become a subject of controversy.

VENUS IN HELPFUL ASPECT WITH NEPTUNE

This aspect promotes peace, contentment, and general goodwill; lessens the conflict between different classes and sectors of society; and brings better conditions for the laboring classes and those in need. Charitable projects flourish, and a general sense of unity becomes widespread.

VENUS CONJUNCT OR IN HOSTILE
ASPECT WITH NEPTUNE

This aspect is unfortunate for every aspect of social life, encouraging class conflict and hatred among different ethnic, religious, and economic groups. It warns of scandals in society, and of fraud and embezzlement in the economic sphere. Political passions become more heated and more unreasonable.

CHAPTER 7

MARS

In traditional mundane astrology, Mars is a malefic planet and warns of approaching trouble, misfortune, and crisis. He is above all else the planet of war. Mars in or ruling an angular house is one of the classic warning signs in mundane astrology, announcing danger of war. If peregrine, an angular Mars indicates a danger of war that will be relatively easy to avert; the more dignified or debilitated that Mars is, and the more planets that are in aspect to him, the harder it will be to prevent conflict from breaking out.

Mars also represents violent crime, epidemic diseases, natural disasters, and political unrest. When well dignified he can represent reform, changes for the better, high-profile criminal prosecutions, and the removal of bad officials and conditions. Now that women have become a significant political force throughout the Western world and in many other countries as well, and Venus has become constellated as the planet of the women's vote and of women's issues, Mars can also represent the men of the nation for which the chart is cast, as well as the men's vote, issues and stances supported principally by men, and of everything else that concerns men collectively in national life.

I have suggested in another book, *The Twilight of Pluto*, that in the future, Mercury rather than Mars will be the significator of masculine energies in astrology, as part of a general reorientation of planetary forces set in motion by the rise and fall of Pluto as a planetary influence. Such changes take time; the gradual way that successful men are gradually separating out into two classes, which we can call "geeks" and "hunks" for convenience, shows that the process still has a long way to run. For now, Mars still seems to do a better job of tracking the masculine influence, but keep an eye on Mercury.

The houses that Mars rules or occupies in a mundane chart indicate the department of the national life that will be a source of crisis and conflict during the period for which the chart is cast. The condition of Mars, in turn, tells you how that department of the national life will be shaped by the crises and conflicts thus indicated.

Alongside the considerations just mentioned, Mars's placements and rulerships in the charts have the following general meanings:

1ST HOUSE

A dignified Mars in or ruling the 1st house gives vigor and strength to the country and enables it to pursue collective goals with focused energy. It is fortunate for the nation and government and often signals some form of national success. It is favorable for men's issues. If the nation is at war, this position makes victory more likely, unless it is shared by both the contending nations.

A debilitated Mars in or ruling the 1st house inspires a bellicose, martial spirit in national affairs, leading politicians and people alike to prefer aggression to more-peaceful methods even when the latter would be more effective. If other indications agree, it can signal the coming of war. It can also warn of domestic unrest, riots, strikes, and an increase in violent crime. If malefic or debilitated planets rule or are placed in the 6th or 8th houses, it can indicate a pandemic.

2ND HOUSE

A dignified Mars in or ruling the 2nd house is favorable for economic affairs, though it often indicates high government expenditure and political intervention in the economy. It can predict economic reforms and changed conditions. Defense industries prosper.

A debilitated Mars in or ruling the 2nd house warns of governmental extravagance and harmful political interference in economic affairs, leading to disaffection and unrest among the people. Stock markets lose ground, investments are unfortunate, bankruptcies increase, and legal tussles over financial issues are common. Beware of any rise in the price of financial investments—it will likely be followed by a sharp decline.

3RD HOUSE

A dignified Mars in or ruling the 3rd house favors new technology and investment in transport, communications, and media. Changes set in motion under this placement will be more likely to turn out well, and investments in 3rd-house industries are favored. Rivalries with neighboring countries will lead to beneficial results.

A debilitated Mars in or ruling the 3rd house brings accidents, strikes, and other forms of disruption to transportation, communication, and media industries. New technologies put to use during this placement will not live up to their apparent promise, and investments will perform poorly due to unexpected events. Airplane crashes and other transport accidents are more common during this time, and so is violence in the schools.

4TH HOUSE

A dignified Mars in or ruling the 4th house favors investments in real estate and reforms in the real estate, agriculture, and mining industries. This is a difficult placement for Mars, however, and unless Mars is very well dignified, it tends to predict bad harvests and turmoil among the common people. The interests of rural people are threatened. Since this house rules the party out of power, it suggests that this party will have success in appealing to the men's vote or to issues that concern men.

A debilitated Mars in or ruling the 4th house warns of drought, bad harvests, and a risk of shortages of foodstuffs. The people are impoverished, discontented, and angry, and the stability of governments is at risk. Fires, accidents, or civil disturbances are likely. It predicts trouble for the party out of power. A troubled Mars in or ruling the 4th house in opposition to the Sun or the ruler of the 10th house indicates a danger of domestic insurgency, revolution, or civil war.

5TH HOUSE

A dignified Mars in or ruling the 5th house is favorable for entertainment, tourism, and speculation, though the benefits may not be long lasting. Movies and other entertainment aimed at a male audience will likely prosper, and so will professional sports. This is the best possible time for a male celebrity-to-be to make his public debut. Since this house also governs the upper house of the legislature, this placement is favorable for reforms and changes affecting that house.

A debilitated Mars in or ruling the 5th house is a bad sign for all 5th-house industries and economic sectors. It predicts trouble in speculative markets and difficult times for tourism and other entertainment industries. As the planet of violence, a debilitated Mars also warns of an increase in crimes related to this house. Avoid speculating when Mars is in this house, since the risk of theft and fraud is increased, while high society will be shaken by scandals and crimes. The upper house of the legislature will be unfortunate and may lose power relative to the lower house or other branches of government.

6TH HOUSE

A dignified Mars in or ruling the 6th house is favorable for the nation's military and for defense industries. It is also favorable for the labor force, giving labor activity increased vigor and success, and strikes and other labor actions during this time will likely succeed. Reforms and new ventures related to public health are also favored by this position.

A debilitated Mars in or ruling the 6th house is the classic warning of epidemic disease. It can also indicate unemployment and poverty, labor troubles, discontent among the working classes, and difficulties affecting the armed forces. New weapons systems will not perform as desired. Look for explosions and fires on the front pages of the news.

7TH HOUSE

A dignified Mars in or ruling the 7th house predicts significant changes in foreign affairs. If Mars is especially well dignified, these changes may be peaceful, but Mars in the 7th under any conditions sounds an alert that war is possible. Challenges in foreign policy will be resolved by decisive action. Bellicose attitudes are common.

A debilitated Mars in or ruling the 7th house is one of the classic indications of impending war. He brings difficulties in foreign affairs, strained relations with other countries, and a serious risk of hostilities between nations. Formerly friendly countries turn hostile, and the nation faces harsh criticism abroad. Crises are unavoidable and may too easily spin out of control.

8TH HOUSE

A dignified Mars in or ruling the 8th house predicts significant changes in foreign trade and investment and is beneficial for defense industries. Unless Mars is very well dignified, however, this is a difficult placement that very often predicts increased illness and death.

A debilitated Mars in or ruling the 8th house is a very negative sign, warning of disease and a sharp rise in the national death rate. Foreign trade and investment are harmed by sudden crises or by military activity abroad. This placement can also indicate riots, civil disturbances, and natural disasters and is almost always followed by the death of important national figures.

9TH HOUSE

A dignified Mars in or ruling the 9th house indicates significant reforms and changes in the legal and religious spheres of society. It is favorable for space travel and for anything else involving travel and exploration at great distances. The nation's high court will rule decisively on issues of importance. International cooperation is emphasized.

A debilitated Mars in or ruling the 9th house announces disputes and turmoil in the religious sphere, controversial court cases, bad legal rulings, and serious trouble with long-distance transport. It can warn of the outbreak of war between other countries that will affect the nation indirectly. If Mars is badly afflicted, this indicates disasters in foreign countries that will affect the country for which the chart is cast; pay attention to the house placement of Mars to see which parts of national life will be affected.

10TH HOUSE

A dignified Mars in or ruling the 10th house strengthens the government and the military and makes the country successful and strong. The party in power will succeed in appealing to male voters and in addressing issues of importance to men. In time of war, this placement indicates victory, and in time of peace it often predicts the settlement of important issues without war breaking out.

A debilitated Mars in or ruling the 10th house is another of the classic signs of imminent war. Bellicose rhetoric is widespread, and hostilities may easily break out. It indicates trouble and anxiety, and the emergence of enemies at home and abroad. It can signal violent protests and rioting or, if very badly afflicted, an attempt to overthrow the government by force. National expenditure is high, and taxation will become a source of public dissatisfaction.

11TH HOUSE

A dignified Mars in or ruling the 11th house gives strength and activity to the government, but there will be significant opposition, and legislative activities will be marked by a quarrelsome and belligerent spirit on all sides. Crises, foreign or domestic, will occupy the attention of the national legislature. Challenges can be overcome with vigorous action.

A debilitated Mars in or ruling the 11th house burdens the national legislature with violent scenes and irreconcilable disagreements. The government will be unable to get its legislative agenda enacted. Angry words and displays of temper will be common, while constructive attention to legislative issues will be rare indeed.

12TH HOUSE

A dignified Mars in or ruling the 12th house brings change and reform to national institutions. It is favorable for all secret activities; the nation's intelligence service will be more successful than usual. This is also a favorable time for changes affecting prisons and hospitals.

A debilitated Mars in or ruling the 12th house threatens national institutions with crisis, perhaps overt, perhaps secret. Secret activities do not prosper, and the nation's intelligence services will be less successful than usual; other countries may enter into secret agreements against the nation's interest, and espionage, sabotage, and criminal activities all become more problematic.

MARS IN ASPECT

Aspects between Mars and the Sun, Moon, Mercury, and Venus are covered in previous chapters.

MARS CONJUNCT OR IN HELPFUL ASPECT WITH JUPITER

This aspect brings constructive changes for organizations of all kinds—government, corporate, and nonprofit. Reforms are less difficult, problems easier to overcome, and resistance to needed change less effective. It attracts public attention to organizational issues. Charitable causes and institutions receive more support.

MARS IN HOSTILE ASPECT WITH JUPITER

This aspect warns of crisis and turmoil for organizations, which are beset by disputes, scandals, and hostile criticism. Public sentiment toward organizations becomes more hostile. Proposed changes are often not well thought out, and in any case attempts at reform face forceful resistance. This aspect can also warn of epidemics or problems with public health.

MARS IN HELPFUL ASPECT WITH SATURN

An aspect of efficiency and constructive effort, this benefits the executive power in every sphere of life. It is especially fortunate for governments, which are able to pursue their goals more effectively. The wheels of national life run smoothly, especially in matters of the houses these planets are placed in or rule.

MARS CONJUNCT OR IN HOSTILE ASPECT WITH SATURN

A difficult aspect, predicting public discontent with the existing order of society. Anger and dissatisfaction drive turbulent events; there is a risk of rioting and of crimes against authority figures. The government loses popularity and support. If other indications support this, it can signal a serious crisis in the nation's affairs.

MARS IN HELPFUL ASPECT WITH URANUS

A very favorable aspect for constructive change and beginnings, this aspect brings energy and success to the nation and is fortunate for any new thing. Under this aspect, legislation is successful and tends to accomplish its goals; difficulties are overcome.

MARS CONJUNCT OR IN HOSTILE
ASPECT WITH URANUS

A disruptive influence bringing on unexpected crises, this aspect is unfortunate for government and nation alike, amplifying disputes and disagreements, igniting quarrels, and encouraging turbulence and lawlessness. If other indications support this, an important figure may die. The political world is shaken.

MARS IN HELPFUL ASPECT WITH NEPTUNE

This is fortunate for the interests of the people. Popular causes make headway, and the people gain power at the expense of the political class. Long-standing problems can sometimes be overcome under this aspect.

MARS CONJUNCT OR IN HOSTILE
ASPECT WITH NEPTUNE

Under this aspect the interests of the people suffer; popular causes encounter forceful opposition from the political class or from within. Scandals attract public attention, and there is much talk of secret crimes and conspiracies. This aspect is also unfortunate for public health and can indicate the coming of an epidemic.

CHAPTER 8

JUPITER

Jupiter is considered a benefic planet. Unless he is seriously afflicted, he brings good fortune to the house or houses in which he is placed, or that he rules, and often brings some benefit even if afflicted. Traditionally he is held to rule religion, clergy, and the churches or other religious institutions in society; he is also assigned the rulership of laws, courts, and judges, as well as charitable organizations.

I have found these rulerships to be correct in modern practice, but incomplete. Jupiter is the planet of hierarchy, and he rules every organization that is set up in a hierarchical manner, whether government, corporate, or nonprofit. He is especially influential in today's corporate sphere, with its quest for constant expansion and its focus on wealth. When well dignified or neutral, he fosters peace, prosperity, order, and profit; when poorly dignified, he encourages stagnation, corruption, and a habit of ignoring problems while they are still small enough to be managed. He is of great importance in economic life and should always be watched for clues to the economic condition of the nation or region under discussion.

The houses that Jupiter rules or occupies in a mundane chart indicate the department of the national life that will see the most expansion, development, or profit during the period for which the chart is cast. The condition of Jupiter, in turn, tells you how growth and expansion in that department of the national life will affect the nation as a whole.

Alongside the considerations just mentioned, Jupiter's placements and rulerships in the charts have the following general meanings:

1ST HOUSE

A dignified Jupiter in or ruling the 1st house is a very favorable indication for the general well-being of the country, predicting prosperity and contentment for the people. It indicates an upturn in economic conditions, increased trade at home and abroad, resolution of conflicts with other countries, and the coming of peace. It is also favorable for religious institutions and for public philanthropy and charity; these receive more support than usual.

A debilitated Jupiter in or ruling the 1st house indicates growth, expansion, and profit for society, but with unexpected drawbacks and difficulties. If the 2nd or 5th house is afflicted, it can warn of unsustainable growth, speculative bubbles, or other situations where gain in the present will be paid for by loss in the future. Under this influence, restraint is thrown to the winds and excesses abound, with results that will be felt later on.

2ND HOUSE

A dignified Jupiter in or ruling the 2nd house is extremely fortunate for the national economy, showing a period of economic expansion, improved trade and commerce, and very often a decrease in the tax burden on individuals and businesses. It benefits everything connected to money matters. Under almost any conditions, Jupiter is very fortunate here.

A debilitated Jupiter in or ruling the 2nd house is still fortunate, but troubled in various ways. If afflicted by one or more planets, the nature of that planet shows the trouble—for example, if afflicted by Mars, government expenditures will be high, and war may interfere with trade; if afflicted by Neptune, a speculative bubble is likely, and so on. Under any circumstances, money will be spent unwisely, and embezzlement and other forms of financial crime are more widespread than usual.

3RD HOUSE

A dignified Jupiter in or ruling the 3rd house brings major benefits to the economic sectors ruled by this house—transport, communications, media, and internet. Travel and tourism increase. Education, literature, and scholarship also benefit from this placement, and new and important scientific discoveries or works of literature are the subject of much attention.

A debilitated Jupiter in or ruling the 3rd house warns of trouble in any or all of these economic sectors. Impending troubles are ignored, and dubious financial dealings are common in these areas. Troubles afflict educational institutions.

4TH HOUSE

A dignified Jupiter in or ruling the 4th house is very favorable for the interests of the ordinary people of the country, who will tend to prosper. Unless other indications suggest the contrary, peace and contentment are widespread and the people hold favorable opinions of those who rule the country. This is an especially fortunate indication for the agricultural sector, predicting a profitable season for farmers and all those connected with them, as well as for resource industries generally. It also predicts rising values for real estate.

A debilitated Jupiter in or ruling the 4th house is still somewhat fortunate, but there will be troubles alongside the good fortune. Profiteering is likely in agriculture and resource industries, and corruption and graft become widespread. This placement also traditionally indicates a risk of a serious earthquake.

5TH HOUSE

A dignified Jupiter in or ruling the 5th house is very favorable for tourism and entertainment industries of all kinds, which will prosper under its influence. It is also favorable for speculative markets and investments. Under this aspect the doings of the rich and famous become more important than usual in the collective thinking of the time.

A debilitated Jupiter in or ruling the 5th house has effects similar to those of a dignified Jupiter in this house, but with downsides that may not be apparent until later. Tourism and entertainment may absorb too large a share of economic activity, at the expense of more-productive sectors, and speculative markets under this influence are likely to get caught up in bubbles and rise to unsustainable levels, resulting in a market crash later on. The doings of the rich and famous monopolize the public attention, resulting in resentment and social conflict.

6TH HOUSE

A dignified Jupiter in or ruling the 6th house predicts better conditions for the laboring classes; wealth is widely distributed in society, wages increase, and jobs are readily available. Public health is good under this influence, and the country's military benefits from improved funding.

A debilitated Jupiter in or ruling the 6th house warns of a bad distribution of income, with too much concentrated in too few hands. Wages rise in some industries but not in others, and there are not enough jobs for the workforce; corruption in employment matters also becomes a significant problem here, and the military is also troubled by financial chicanery. Public health is bad and the hospitals are full; respiratory illnesses and diseases affecting the liver are common.

7TH HOUSE

A dignified Jupiter in or ruling the 7th house is an excellent sign for foreign affairs, announcing a period of friendly relations with other nations. If this placement occurs during a war, efforts to negotiate peace will be greatly strengthened; if it occurs in a time of peace, war is very unlikely. Treaties, alliances, and commercial agreements are likely, and those negotiated or signed while this placement is in effect will be beneficial for all parties.

A debilitated Jupiter in or ruling the 7th house is still an indication of peace and friendly relations, but with significant problems or costs attached. Agreements made between countries while this placement applies will turn out to have unnoticed downsides; in time of war, peace agreements negotiated will be broken or will place the country at a disadvantage, and so on.

8TH HOUSE

A dignified Jupiter in or ruling the 8th house is very favorable for foreign trade and investment. Trade agreements negotiated under this influence will be profitable for the country, the balance of trade will improve, and foreign investment will be put to good use. The death rate will decline.

A debilitated Jupiter in or ruling the 8th house predicts excessive dependence on foreign trade and investment, with economic problems likely to follow. Corruption of politicians and business leaders by foreign money is likely. The death rate increases, and celebrity deaths with a significant impact on popular culture are likely.

9TH HOUSE

A dignified Jupiter in or ruling the 9th house is a good omen for the national judiciary. Important court cases are resolved in ways that benefit society and are widely seen as just and fair. In societies with strong religious traditions, this is equally favorable for religious institutions, which expand their influence. A nation with a space program or some other advanced scientific or technological project is likely to achieve some significant milestone under this placement.

A debilitated Jupiter in or ruling the 9th house can expect bad rulings from its national judiciary, with corruption of judges or less overt bias toward wealthy interests on display. Religious institutions abuse their power and wealth, and corruption is equally likely in this setting. Money spent on advanced scientific or technological projects such as space travel will be wasted.

10TH HOUSE

A dignified Jupiter in or ruling the 10th house is a very favorable sign for the executive branch of the national government. The country can expect peace and prosperity, and increased tax revenues for government due to economic expansion make it easy for the government to pursue its agenda and win the approval of the population. It brings success to the nation and its leaders, and important new national projects are likely to be launched under its influence.

A debilitated Jupiter in or ruling the 10th house remains favorable for the executive branch but, again, with drawbacks and costs. Excessive expenditure by the government is likely, and financial commitments made at this time may prove too costly later on. As always with an afflicted Jupiter, corruption is likely. Social and political problems are ignored rather than being addressed.

11TH HOUSE

A dignified Jupiter in or ruling the 11th house benefits the legislative branch of government and especially the lower house of the national legislature. Friendly relations with other countries are favored by this placement, and new laws and bills passed while this influence is in place will prove to be beneficial to the country. Legislation proceeds smoothly, partisan discord decreases, and new benefits and rights are conferred on the people.

A debilitated Jupiter in or ruling the 11th house makes the national legislature, and especially the lower house, more concerned with the personal profits of its members than with issues confronting the nation. Under this placement, expect graft and corruption in politics on an unusually large scale, while important issues are neglected and problems mount up out of view of the political establishment. Apparent good times conceal rising pressures that will lead to serious trouble later on.

12TH HOUSE

A dignified Jupiter in or ruling the 12th house is fortunate for all the institutions of national life. The nonprofit sector thrives, funding for charitable and beneficial enterprises is ample, and public attention focuses on the needs of the poor and unfortunate. A wealthy or influential person sets an example by donating large sums to charity.

A debilitated Jupiter in or ruling the 12th house warns of financial crimes and inappropriate abuses of wealth and power in the institutional and nonprofit sector. Wealth meant for charitable and beneficial enterprises is misused for other purposes. Institutions take on commitments they will not be able to meet in the longer term.

JUPITER IN ASPECT

Jupiter's aspects with the luminaries and the inner planets are covered in previous chapters.

JUPITER IN HELPFUL ASPECT
WITH SATURN

A very favorable aspect for the national economy, since it combines wealth and hard work. Government finances improve, and taxes may be reduced if other indications agree. Practical measures are put in place to benefit national prosperity.

JUPITER CONJUNCT OR IN HOSTILE
ASPECT WITH SATURN

A problematic aspect but very hard to pin down, since the unwelcome news it brings can take many different shapes. Some form of economic trouble can be expected, and the government faces difficulties it may not be able to overcome. Bad policies or regulations are likely to be enacted.

JUPITER IN HELPFUL
ASPECT WITH URANUS

A favorable aspect for constructive legislation, this predicts helpful reforms and new laws that will benefit society. It strengthens the party in power and predicts peace, good government, and improved conditions.

JUPITER CONJUNCT OR IN HOSTILE
ASPECT WITH URANUS

Under this aspect, watch for new laws and regulations that cause more problems than they solve, and reforms that prove unworkable in practice. It is unfortunate for the party in power and for everyone in positions in authority. In wartime, defeat is likely.

JUPITER IN HELPFUL
ASPECT WITH NEPTUNE

An aspect of peace and goodwill, this benefits the people as a whole, and especially those who are unfortunate or disadvantaged. Humanitarian movements meet with success under this aspect. Disputes between nations find peaceful settlement. This aspect also benefits religious organizations and movements.

JUPITER CONJUNCT OR IN HOSTILE ASPECT WITH NEPTUNE

Confusion, misunderstanding, and charges of bad faith are likely under this aspect, which disturbs peace and order. Conflict between the political class and the masses is likely. Watch for public excitement over mysterious or secret crimes; conspiracy theories flourish, and if other indications support this, so do conspiracies.

CHAPTER 9

SATURN

In traditional mundane astrology, Saturn is the planet of hard facts, hard knocks, and the things that endure. He is the great limiting factor among the planets, imposing order, setting boundaries, establishing those things that have the capacity to last, and tipping old and outworn elements of national life into history's dumpster. When he is well dignified, he promises stability, calm, and the sort of prosperity that comes not from growth but from wise management of existing resources. When he is debilitated, he warns of difficult times, painful events, and the unwanted consequences of past behavior. He is traditionally the Greater Malefic, so be warned: negative Saturn placements and aspects tend to bring more grief than almost anything else in a mundane chart.

The houses that Saturn rules or occupies in a mundane chart indicate the aspects of the national life that will be subject to hard limits or dependent on enduring realities during the period for which the chart is cast. The condition of Saturn, in turn, tells you how those limits and realties will play out over the period of the chart, as a source of strengths or of weakness.

Alongside the considerations just mentioned, Saturn's placements and rulerships in the charts have the following general meanings:

1ST HOUSE

A dignified Saturn in or ruling the 1st house promises a calm and prosperous time for the nation and its people. Governments are better behaved than usual, and the business climate allows the nation's wealth to spread more evenly. The nation experiences some notable success, not through dramatic action but by patient and prudent management.

A debilitated Saturn in or ruling the 1st house brings the government and the political classes into disrepute. Public discontent spreads, the government faces sharp criticism, and poverty and crime are widespread. Pay attention to aspects affecting Saturn in this placement, for hostile aspects with another planet can indicate the death or disgrace of a nationally important figure.

2ND HOUSE

A dignified Saturn in or ruling the 2nd house is a favorable economic indicator; the nation prospers due to prudent policies and cautious management. Stability replaces volatility, and investment money moves into productive industries and economic sectors.

A debilitated Saturn in or ruling the 2nd house brings economic contraction and increased poverty. If other indicators support this, a recession or depression is possible. Business failures increase, stocks and other investments decline in value, and taxation increases.

3RD HOUSE

A dignified Saturn in or ruling the 3rd house predicts relative stability in the economic sectors relating to this house. Established firms in transport, communications, and the media perform better than startups. This is a favorable time for long-term investments in these sectors.

A debilitated Saturn in or ruling the 3rd house brings hard times and diminished prospects to the transport, communications, and media sectors of the economy. Shares of companies in this sector decline in value, and firms do not prosper. Labor relations become difficult, and charges of mismanagement are likely.

4TH HOUSE

A dignified Saturn in or ruling the 4th house is moderately favorable for agriculture and resource industries; production and prices both remain steady, and established interests in these sectors do well. Real estate prices are stable. Peace and contentment prevails in the rural hinterlands. The party out of power embraces a more conservative approach to politics.

A debilitated Saturn in or ruling the 4th house is a very unfortunate sign, predicting trouble for the government and the nation as a whole. Unemployment, poverty, and dissatisfaction become widespread, especially in the rural hinterlands. Agriculture, resource industries, and real estate all lose ground. The party out of power is no better off than the one in power and is beset by crises of its own.

5TH HOUSE

A dignified Saturn in or ruling the 5th house is still moderately unfavorable, since 5th-house interests do not thrive under Saturn's influence. Entertainment, tourism, and speculative markets face, at best, stable and predictable conditions. The upper house of the national legislature accomplishes little but at least does no harm.

A debilitated Saturn in or ruling the 5th house is another very bad omen, predicting hard times for the entertainment and tourism sectors and a prolonged downturn for speculative markets. Some collective event casts a shadow over the national mood; the death of a respected national figure may bring a time of national mourning.

6TH HOUSE

A dignified Saturn in or ruling the 6th house is a favorable sign, bringing stable conditions for the laboring classes and also for public health. Prudent policies are enacted in one or both of these fields. In military affairs this is favorable for defensive measures, such as the construction of fortifications, and also for establishing new military bases.

A debilitated Saturn in or ruling the 6th house is a bad sign for public health. Expect chronic illnesses to increase and average life spans to decline. If Saturn is afflicted by another planet, a disease corresponding in character to that planet will become more widespread—for example, a feverish illness if Mars is afflicting, or a sexually transmitted illness if Venus afflicts. Discontent and unemployment spread among the laboring classes. The military faces troubles; in wartime, this can indicate a serious defeat.

7TH HOUSE

A dignified Saturn in or ruling the 7th house is a very favorable sign, predicting peace and stability in international affairs. This is a fortunate time for creating and strengthening alliances abroad, resolving difficulties, overcoming hostility, and establishing favorable economic and political relationships.

A debilitated Saturn in or ruling the 7th house is less favorable. Stability reigns and war is unlikely, unless other indications contradict, but hostilities become entrenched, international relations are subject to coldness and jealousy, attempts at negotiations fail, and political and economic affairs are troubled by difficulties abroad.

8TH HOUSE

A dignified Saturn in or ruling the 8th house is a good indication for foreign investment and trade. This is a favorable time for trade agreements and economic cooperation between nations, as well as for investment abroad. As with other favorable Saturn placements, stability and peace are indicated, and prudence and cautious management are advantageous.

A debilitated Saturn in or ruling the 8th house warns of a decline in foreign investment and trade, with lasting negative economic consequences. Since the 8th is also the traditional sign of death, an afflicted Saturn in or ruling this house can also predict an increase in mortality and very often signals deaths from disease and poverty.

9TH HOUSE

A dignified Saturn in or ruling the 9th house favors judicial rulings that maintain peace and public order. The laws will be more fairly enforced. It also brings success to conservative religious movements.

A debilitated Saturn in or ruling the 9th house predicts harsh and unpopular judicial rulings of a conservative or reactionary nature. The laws are harshly and unfairly enforced, leading to conflict in society. This placement is also traditionally associated with accidents affecting air or space travel, troubles with long-distance transport of all kinds, and storms or collisions at sea.

10TH HOUSE

A dignified Saturn in or ruling the 10th house gives strength to the political establishment, but not popularity. The government and the country overcome difficulties, at least in the short term. Public order is maintained and the system of government remains firmly in place.

A debilitated Saturn in or ruling the 10th house is a very bad sign for the government and the nation. It predicts a loss of popularity or even a crisis of legitimacy for the party or government in power. Serious difficulties mount up, discord spreads through the affairs of the nation, and plain bad luck afflicts the government. If other indications support, this can signal the death of an important political figure.

11TH HOUSE

A dignified Saturn in or ruling the 11th house is favorable for the national legislature and especially for the lower house. Legislative business proceeds in a steady, patient, and careful manner. The government is secure and, given prudent management, may achieve some important success. If this aspect affects an election, unless other indications contradict, the party in power will hold its own.

A debilitated Saturn in or ruling the 11th house predicts delay, obstruction, and discord in the legislative process. Bills fail or are delayed in passage, the parties are unable to compromise, and public discontent with the national legislature is widespread. If this aspect affects an election, unless other indications contradict, the party in power will do very poorly.

12TH HOUSE

A dignified Saturn in or ruling the 12th house exercises a steadying influence on the nonprofit sector and the nation's institutions and can indicate improved management and new regulations. Saturn is always troubled in this house, however, and so at best there will be only very modest problems in the institutional sector.

A debilitated Saturn in or ruling the 12th house warns of serious problems for the institutions of national life and for the nonprofit sector as a whole. It also warns of a loss of power or prestige on the part of important figures in government, or of the government as a whole. The national interest suffers due to the activities of organized crime or of foreign espionage and subversion.

SATURN IN ASPECT

Aspects between Saturn and every planet but Uranus and Neptune have been covered in earlier chapters.

SATURN IN HELPFUL ASPECT WITH URANUS

When the planets of stability and revolutionary change are in favorable aspect, constructive reform and orderly change are in the air. This aspect supports the party in power, inspiring strong and fair leadership. It is favorable for new legislation; if the Sun or Jupiter is in helpful aspect to either planet or otherwise provides support, great reforms and transformations can take place without struggle.

SATURN CONJUNCT OR IN HOSTILE ASPECT WITH URANUS

In almost any other relationship, by contrast, these two planets conflict forcefully and inspire epic struggles. This aspect is very unfortunate for the government and the party in power, piling up troubles and crises that have no quick solution. If other indications support this, an important political figure may die. Opposition, delay, and difficulty beset every attempt at constructive change.

SATURN IN HELPFUL ASPECT WITH NEPTUNE

This aspect brings new laws and reforms that benefit the people and the causes that concern them. The popular interest gains strength. This also benefits the national economy, bringing stability and a steady improvement in conditions.

SATURN CONJUNCT OR IN HOSTILE
ASPECT WITH NEPTUNE

An aspect of disorganization, confusion, and delay, this aspect causes difficulties throughout national life, though it is focused on the houses in which the planets rule or are placed. Some serious loss affects the nation, and authority figures face discredit or downfall.

CHAPTER 10

URANUS

Uranus is the first of the planets we are surveying that had no place in traditional mundane astrology, because he had not yet been discovered when the classic methods of mundane interpretation were created. Many astrologers today suggest that newly discovered planets represent influences that were not active in human affairs until the time of their discovery. In modern mundane charts, certainly, Uranus is a potent force.

He is the planet of the individual, of democracy, and of countercultures and alternative movements in society. He is particularly the planet of alternative sexualities—for many years, in fact, the word "Uranian" was a synonym for "gay"—and of gender identities other than male and female. He also governs invention and discovery. Whereas Mercury rules tools and crafts that require skilled human input, Uranus governs technologies that run with little or no human input; he is the ruler of machines, factories, computers, and the internet. He always brings radical change, and when badly dignified he signals crises, conflict, and revolution.

The houses that Uranus rules or occupies in a mundane chart indicate the department of the national life that will face significant disruptive change during the period governed by the chart. The condition of Uranus, in turn, tells you whether the Uranian influence will be constructive or destructive in that part of national life.

Alongside the considerations just mentioned, Uranus's placements and rulerships in the charts have the following general meanings:

1ST HOUSE

A dignified Uranus in or ruling the 1st house indicates that positive changes can be expected in the national life. This placement strengthens the government and encourages reforms and new ventures on a national level. Some significant national success can be expected during a period influenced by this placement.

A debilitated Uranus in or ruling the 1st house brings discontent, dissatisfaction, and turmoil. The government and, in particular, the national legislature will face trouble and discord. Protests, strikes, riots, and, if other indications support this, armed rebellion all are possible. If Uranus is afflicted by malefics, the public imagination focuses on shocking crimes.

2ND HOUSE

A dignified Uranus in or ruling the 2nd house, if free of all hostile influences, can indicate unexpected prosperity and constructive reforms in matters affecting the economy. Even slight debility, however, brings turmoil and a risk of economic crisis.

A debilitated Uranus in or ruling the 2nd house causes volatility and disruption in economic matters. He warns of financial crises, downside movement in stocks and other investment markets, and confusion and disruption to business affairs. If other indications support this, he can herald the coming of a recession.

3RD HOUSE

A dignified Uranus in or ruling the 3rd house favors discoveries, inventions, new technologies, and scientific achievements. Industries in this house will experience rapid change. The national legislature will pass measures that benefit this sector.

A debilitated Uranus in or ruling the 3rd house warns of accidents, disruptions, or crises caused by technology and innovation. New ventures will be unfortunate and unexpected problems will arise in the introduction of novel technologies. Transportation bottlenecks are likely.

4TH HOUSE

A dignified Uranus in or ruling the 4th house brings constructive change to 4th-house interests. It is especially favorable for resource industries, such as fossil fuel production or rare-earth mining, and for significant changes in land use. Legislation affecting real estate, agriculture, and other 4th-house industries is likely to be fortunate. The party out of power benefits by reforms, reorganization, and new ventures.

A debilitated Uranus in or ruling the 4th house brings trouble and discredit on the national legislature and the government as a whole. This placement is unfavorable for agriculture and other 4th-house interests. If badly afflicted and near the cusp, there is a risk of a damaging earthquake. Accidents, explosions, and mine cave-ins are possible. The party out of power suffers due to internal strife and failures of leadership.

5TH HOUSE

A dignified Uranus in or ruling the 5th house is favorable for new ventures and innovations in tourism and the entertainment industries. Avant-garde, original, and unexpected movements in art, theater, and other entertainment media are more likely to thrive. Speculative markets benefit, but the big gains will come in unlikely and unpredictable places.

A debilitated Uranus in or ruling the 5th house brings trouble to the entertainment industries. New movies and television shows perform below expectations. Strikes and other labor troubles in these industries are likely. Disagreements and scandals can be expected in high society. Speculative markets are troubled and volatile, and if other indications support this, a crash is possible.

6TH HOUSE

A dignified Uranus in or ruling the 6th house brings beneficial changes to public health and to the condition of the laboring classes. New legislation on either or both of these matters is likely. The military benefits from adopting new technology or tactics, or from reorganization. Public health is unstable but may improve.

A debilitated Uranus in or ruling the 6th house is a very bad indication for public health and may indicate an epidemic or some other increase in sickness. The laboring classes are dissatisfied with their conditions; strikes and other workplace troubles can be expected. The military faces a difficult time, and any new technology, tactics, or organizational measures brought in while this placement applies will turn out to be far more trouble than they are worth.

7TH HOUSE

A dignified Uranus in or ruling the 7th house is favorable for foreign policy. Significant changes in foreign affairs are likely, and new treaties and agreements with other nations signed while this placement is in effect will have unexpected positive results. In wartime, this placement can be an indication of victory; under any conditions, it brings power, influence, and success.

A debilitated Uranus in or ruling the 7th house warns of crisis, complications, and difficulties in foreign affairs. Sudden changes bring troubles on the nation; enmity and rivalry between nations are widespread.

Treaties and agreements are broken or turn out to be disadvantageous. In wartime, this often indicates defeat on the battlefield.

8TH HOUSE

A dignified Uranus in or ruling the 8th house brings significant changes in foreign trade and investment. Innovative technologies are favored in affairs of this house. It is a favorable time to make trade agreements and to pursue investments abroad. Legislation affecting 8th-house issues is likely to have good results.

A debilitated Uranus in or ruling the 8th house announces trouble for the nation's foreign trade and its investments abroad. Sudden political shifts may cause serious disruptions and financial losses in matters of this house. Treaties and legislation affecting foreign trade and investment will have unexpected negative consequences. Since the 8th house is also traditionally the house of death, the national death rate increases; an epidemic or some other cause of widespread death is likely. If other indications support this, the head of government may die.

9TH HOUSE

A dignified Uranus in or ruling the 9th house is favorable for judicial reforms and court decisions increasing individual liberty and defending the rights of the individual against the state. It also favors new religions and religious innovation, and advances in air travel, space travel, and other technologies focused on things at great distance can be expected.

A debilitated Uranus in or ruling the 9th house warns of failed judicial reforms and bad decisions handed down by the courts. Religious denominations are troubled by dissent and schism. This is an unfortunate time for innovations of all kinds.

10TH HOUSE

A dignified Uranus in or ruling the 10th house favors the central government, lending it strength and activity. Very often this placement is associated with some significant national success at home or abroad. Important political reforms are likely.

A debilitated Uranus in or ruling the 10th house brings serious trouble on the government, which faces unpopularity and discontent among the people. Reforms made at this time will fail to achieve their goals and will likely be unpopular as well. If other indications support this, the government may fall from power, or the head of government may die.

11TH HOUSE

A dignified Uranus in or ruling the 11th house is favorable for legislative activity. New laws are enacted, reforms take place, and sweeping changes affect the country. The national legislature is active and important issues are dealt with.

A debilitated Uranus in or ruling the 11th house brings turmoil and disruption to the national legislature. Sudden changes take place, important bills are delayed or fail, and unwise reforms cause trouble and hardship. This placement is unfortunate for the party in power, and if an election takes place during it, a change of leadership in the legislature is likely.

12TH HOUSE

A dignified Uranus in or ruling the 12th house brings new legislation, regulations, and reforms to the institutions of national life. It is also favorable for reforms and new laws affecting criminal justice. The nation's espionage services are successful.

A debilitated Uranus in or ruling the 12th house brings disruptive changes to the institutions of national life. Mysterious or complicated crimes seize the national imagination. The nation's enemies are successful in espionage or other secret hostilities.

URANUS IN ASPECT

The only aspects of Uranus not already covered in previous chapters are those with Neptune.

URANUS IN HELPFUL ASPECT WITH NEPTUNE

An aspect of harmony between the political class and the people, this strengthens the government and gives it increased popular support. It furthers reforms that benefit the people. Far-reaching constructive changes are likely while this aspect is in effect.

URANUS CONJUNCT OR IN HOSTILE ASPECT WITH NEPTUNE

This aspect, by contrast, guarantees turmoil, disruption, conflict, and interference. The government is shaken, and important political figures may lose power. Attempted reforms will bog down amid a storm of confusion and opposition. Very little will be accomplished, though vast amounts of noise will be produced by the attempt.

CHAPTER 11

NEPTUNE

Neptune is the second planet we are surveying that had no place in traditional mundane astrology, because he had not yet been discovered when the classic methods of mundane interpretation were created. In modern mundane charts, Neptune is a very potent influence, even more potent than Uranus in some ways, and his influence is almost always malefic. A hostile aspect between the Sun and Neptune, in particular, is the single most dangerous indication in a mundane chart.

This may seem surprising; it certainly surprised me when I first started casting mundane charts and compared their predictions to the events that followed. It follows, however, from Neptune's nature. Neptune is the planet of unity, as Uranus is the planet of individuality. He represents unities of all kinds, from the divine unity attained by religious mystics to the bestial unity of a crazed mob on a rampage. The worlds of politics and economics are rarely favorable to unities of any kind, however—movements toward unity in these fields too often trigger a plunge to the lowest common denominator of social life—and so when Neptune is strong, trouble usually follows.

The exceptions occur when Neptune is completely unafflicted and in favorable aspects to other planets. In this condition he favors democratic causes and benefits the masses, for he is the planet of mass phenomena, and an indication of peace within and between nations. In any other condition, he brings chaos, instability, mass movements, fads, fashions, popular crazes, speculative bubbles, defeat, collapse, downfall, and everything else that brings things down to the lowest level. He also warns of scandal, deception, and illusion.

The houses that Neptune rules or occupies in a mundane chart indicate the department of the national life that will have to deal with mass phenomena during the period for which the chart is cast. The condition of Neptune, in turn, tells you how that department of the national life will be shaped by those mass phenomena.

Alongside the considerations just mentioned, Neptune's placements and rulerships in the charts have the following general meanings:

1ST HOUSE

A dignified Neptune in or ruling the 1st house brings popular concerns and mass movements to the fore in national life and provides them additional support and strength. Under this placement, such movements can bring significant benefits to the nation, focusing especially on matters of the house in which Neptune is placed.

A debilitated Neptune in or ruling the 1st house stirs up discontent among the people toward the existing order of society and causes many changes and uncertainties in the affairs of the nation. Mass movements seek power and may gain it if other indications concur. A time of turmoil, unrest, and trouble is indicated. Popular delusions and public scandals are likely.

2ND HOUSE

A dignified Neptune in or ruling the 2nd house brings financial benefits to the people and to popular causes and mass movements. It can also signal popular fads and fancies that turn out to benefit the economic side of society.

A debilitated Neptune in or ruling the 2nd house brings economic trouble through volatility in the markets, mistaken economic policies, false expectations, and outright delusions. Frauds and swindles are common and cause much economic damage. Government finances are a source of trouble. Speculative bubbles are possible, and any sudden increase in the value of investments should be regarded with suspicion.

3RD HOUSE

A dignified Neptune in or ruling the 3rd house is favorable for all 3rd-house industries that deal directly with the public. Fads and fashions benefit those industries that can cash in on them. Favorable for travel and for mass communications technologies such as the internet.

A debilitated Neptune in or ruling the 3rd house brings trouble, discontent, and dissension affecting 3rd-house industries. New ventures in communications, transport, and media fail, often because the public mood unaccountably rejects them. Sensational rumors and false reports in the media cause damage and disruption.

4TH HOUSE

A dignified Neptune in or ruling the 4th house is generally favorable for agriculture and resource industries, and for real estate. It strengthens the political power of the people and of democratic causes and organizations. Mass support for popular movements can be expected under this placement. The party out of power attracts a larger public following.

A debilitated Neptune in or ruling the 4th house causes problems for the government, stirs up disaffection and resistance to government programs, and signals public opposition to the party in power. Failure, scandal, and trouble afflict important political or cultural figures. The party out of power risks being caught up in a mass movement contrary to its interests.

5TH HOUSE

A dignified Neptune in or ruling the 5th house benefits entertainment industries and tourism, encouraging popular fads and fashions that bring money to this sector. The wealthy classes receive public adulation. Speculative investments become popular.

A debilitated Neptune in or ruling the 5th house is the classic indication of a speculative bubble or some other self-terminating craze in business affairs. Expect more than the usual volume of losses, scandals, and illegal activity in the investment world. Scandal and crime beset the wealthy classes and cause a public outcry.

6TH HOUSE

A dignified Neptune in or ruling the 6th house directs the interest and concern of the masses toward public health or the condition of the laboring classes. It can inspire health fads, but so long as Neptune has no afflictions at all, these are unlikely to do much harm. Fads and fashions in military affairs are likely.

A debilitated Neptune in or ruling the 6th house predicts serious problems for public health; it is one of the placements that can warn of a pandemic. It drives dissatisfaction and rebelliousness among the laboring classes, indicates a high risk of strikes and labor actions, and can predict riots and rebellion if other factors concur. In military affairs an afflicted Neptune is a very bad indication, suggesting that the nation's military is deceived or self-deceived about the threats facing it, and risks suffering disastrous surprises when war comes.

7TH HOUSE

A dignified Neptune in or ruling the 7th house is a favorable indication for foreign affairs. It fosters peace and goodwill between nations, encourages a sense of unity, and strengthens international organizations, especially those of an idealistic nature.

A debilitated Neptune in or ruling the 7th house warns of deception and treachery abroad. Seemingly friendly nations may be pursuing hostile policies in secret. Foreign affairs are troubled and uncertain, and policies founded on deception, self-deception, or falsehood are likely to come to grief. Scandals can be expected in this area of the national life.

8TH HOUSE

A dignified Neptune in or ruling the 8th house is favorable for foreign trade and investment. The nation may be united by the death of an important figure or by a public funeral.

A debilitated Neptune in or ruling the 8th house is another very bad indication for public health. It can predict a pandemic or some other factor driving increases in the national death rate; it also warns of new difficulties involving the illegal drug trade. Foreign trade and investment are troubled. Watch for speculative booms and busts abroad spreading financial trouble to the domestic economy.

9TH HOUSE

A dignified Neptune in or ruling the 9th house is very favorable for religion, emphasizing its mystical and personal side at the expense of its institutional side. Peaceful relations among different faiths are highlighted. Court rulings can be expected to set important precedents.

A debilitated Neptune in or ruling the 9th house warns of religious manias and mass movements and of scandals and frauds in religious circles. Court rulings are misguided or harmful.

10TH HOUSE

A dignified Neptune in or ruling the 10th house, if it is completely free from affliction, wins mass support for the government and strengthens democratic and populist movements. It is favorable for national unity.

A debilitated Neptune in or ruling the 10th house puts the masses and the government at odds, warns that the government will lose power or popularity, and can lead to the removal of a head of state or the replacement of the current government by vote or otherwise. Scandal and disgrace affect important political or cultural figures.

11TH HOUSE

A dignified Neptune in or ruling the 11th house is favorable for legislative affairs. It encourages compromise and negotiation between the parties and leads to legislation that is broadly popular. It benefits democratic and populist factions in political life.

A debilitated Neptune in or ruling the 11th house brings confusion, disruption, discord, and delay into legislative affairs. One or more parties may struggle with internal splits, and partisan hatreds are amplified. Very often, under this placement, legislation bogs down and even the most necessary bills cannot be passed.

12TH HOUSE

A dignified Neptune in or ruling the 12th house strengthens national institutions by giving them popular support and associating them with widely held ideals. It is especially favorable for all charitable and humanitarian institutions.

A debilitated Neptune in or ruling the 12th house brings frauds, scandals, and criminal activity to light in national institutions. It is often also associated with espionage and foreign influence, and with charges of treachery or secret enmity between nations.

NEPTUNE IN ASPECT

All the aspects Neptune makes with other planets have been covered in earlier chapters.

CHAPTER 12

THE DWARF PLANETS

With the dwarf planets—Ceres, Pluto, Eris, and any others that might be discovered farther out beyond Neptune—we are venturing into controversial territory. To be more precise, the dwarf planet Pluto is the source of the controversy. Not many people get bent out of shape over the role of Ceres or Eris in mundane charts, but Pluto exercises a weird and frankly unwholesome fascination on the modern mind, and not only in mundane astrology.

I have never found it necessary or even helpful to include the dwarf planets in my mundane predictions. Quite the contrary, I have found that they belong to the class of minor indications that distract attention from more-important factors and lead to less accurate predictions. Nonetheless I have included them here for the sake of completeness, and because readers may find them more useful than I do. We'll survey them one at a time.

CERES

The largest body in the asteroid belt and the only one with gravity powerful enough to draw it into a sphere, Ceres was discovered in 1801. Mistaken at first for a planet, she was downgraded to asteroid status in the 1850s and raised to new dignity as a dwarf planet in 2006. Her rulership and other sign correspondences remain disputed at this point, but she was assigned the rulership of Virgo by astrologers not long after her discovery. In my astrological practice, I have found that this appears to work well, and she is therefore in detriment in Pisces. In my experience the theory that she is exalted in Gemini, and in her fall in Sagittarius, also works well. Further research may require these tentative attributions to be changed, of course.

Astrologically she is the dwarf planet of nutrition and nurturing. In natal charts, her strength is, among other things, a good measure of the role that food and nurturing will play in the native's life. In mundane charts, she could be taken as a significant indication of changes in a nation's food supply and its ability to nurture and support the more vulnerable members of its population. Watch especially the aspects she makes with the outer planets; favorable aspects can predict beneficial changes in these areas, while hostile aspects can predict hard times or outright famine. Mundane charts for nations that have trouble gaining access to adequate food might well pay close attention to Ceres when she is strongly placed by sign, house, or aspect.

PLUTO

The innermost large object in the Kuiper Belt, the vast ring of icy fragments that reaches out beyond Neptune toward the borders of interstellar space, Pluto was discovered in 1930 and, like Ceres, was mistaken at first for a planet. He was downgraded to dwarf planet status in 2006 after decades of research showed that he did not qualify for planetary status by any of the usual measures. During his time as a planet, he was assigned the rulership of Scorpio, and he should probably be given corulership of that sign; his detriment is in Taurus. His exaltation and fall are the subject of some disagreement, but Ivy Goldstein-Jacobson, whose assignments have always produced good results for me, assigned him Aquarius for his exaltation and Leo for his fall.

Pluto has a significant role in mundane astrology, but it's a negative one. If you've been watching internet forums where people try to predict the future by using astrology, you'll likely have seen any number of lurid forecasts based on Pluto's movement through the signs and his aspects with other outer planets. Any number of dire catastrophes, sinister conspiracies, economic crashes, and impending dooms have been blamed on this inoffensive snowball of a worldlet, 1/400th the size of our Earth, swinging through its eccentric orbit on the inner edge of the Kuiper Belt.

The one thing these predictions have in common is that nearly all of them have flopped. What makes this even stranger is that the mere fact that so many of these predictions turn out false somehow never dents the conviction that the next set of wild Plutonian prophecies must surely come to pass. I've come to think that a new rule needs to be added to the traditional precepts of mundane astrology: *There is no easier way to come up with inaccurate predictions and make a fool of yourself than by relying on Pluto.*

This effect can be useful to keep in mind for predictive purposes. In mundane terms, I would suggest, Pluto might best be interpreted as the dwarf planet of overblown hype and fringe-group hysteria. Watch where Pluto is and what aspects he makes to other planets, and you may be able to catch some idea of the themes that will seize the imaginations of the unwary and lead them to make wrong predictions and mistaken pronouncements. More broadly, as an object on the outer edges of the solar system, straying across the boundary line traced by Neptune, he is the dwarf planet of the transgressive social fringes; he rules the criminal underworld, secret societies, and eccentric sects of all kinds. When he is in aspect to an important planet in a mundane chart, he can announce that such groups may play an outsized role in the political or economic scene, or that the private obsession of some such group may become the focus of general attention for a shorter or longer period.

I have argued in my book *The Twilight of Pluto* that Pluto did in fact function as a planet from 1930, the time of his discovery, to 2006, the point at which his insignificant size and influence on the solar system forced astronomers to admit that he was a minor body after all. Analyses of mundane charts from between these days might reasonably take Pluto seriously as a planetary force, though even there—as case study 1 a little further on will show—predictions based on Pluto have had a long track record of going disastrously awry. In my own practice as a mundane astrologer, I have generally found it best to leave Pluto out entirely, as one of those minor factors that confuse prediction rather than assisting it.

There is at least one other possibility worth pursuing, however. Isabel Hickey, one of the most thoughtful of twentieth-century American astrologers, predicted in 1973 on astrological grounds that Pluto would turn out to be a double planet (scientists had to wait several more years before the discovery of the giant moon Charon proved that she was right). Hickey named Pluto's hidden twin planet Minerva, after the goddess of wisdom, and noted that in her readings she found that clients facing a Pluto transit or progression had two options: they could resonate with the largely destructive influences of Pluto or the far more positive influences of Minerva. The choice was quite literally theirs.

Political and economic affairs in the real world are rarely blessed with any noticeable amount of wisdom. Nonetheless it may be worth exploring the possibility, when Pluto is strongly placed in an ingress or eclipse chart, that the nations thus challenged may be able to exercise some choice concerning how the Plutonian/Minervan influence will affect them.

ERIS

Discovered only in 2005, the dwarf planet Eris has been the subject of intensive astrological research since her existence was first announced, but her effects are still too poorly known to allow her to be assigned a definite rulership or meaning in mundane charts. So far she seems to have an affinity for rebelliousness and disruption, but decades of close attention to her effects will be needed before her rulerships, dignities, and debilities can be properly assigned and her influence tracked in mundane charts. This is a field where systematic work by mundane astrologers can contribute significantly to the advance of astrological knowledge.

OTHER BODIES

Over the last century or so, innovative astrologers have proposed meanings for a great many other small bodies and theoretical points in the solar system. I have not found these to be useful as a source of accurate predictions, but your experience may differ from mine. If you are drawn to exploring other bodies or points in a mundane context, by all means do so, but remember to balance your enthusiasm for your research with the need to produce accurate forecasts. Your clients or readers may make important life decisions on the basis of your delineations, after all, and you owe it to them to make predictions that are as accurate as possible—whether or not your predictions factor in your favorite minor bodies or correspond to what you would like to see.

PART 2

CASE STUDIES

CASE STUDY 1

TWO FAMOUS FAILURES

It's only fair to note that mundane astrology can be done badly. To make sense of its current situation, and to offer guidance to prospective mundane astrologers, it may be helpful to start with one of history's most famous examples of a mundane prediction that went very, very wrong, and talk about the reasons why.

In the spring of 1939, C. E. O. Carter was one of the most reputable astrologers in the world, the editor of the popular quarterly *Astrology* and a leading figure in British astrological circles. Thus, most people interested in astrology paid attention when he insisted, at the Harrogate astrological conference in the spring of 1939, that the stars predicted peace in Europe rather than war for the rest of that year. He was, of course, disastrously wrong. His highly publicized mistake dealt a body blow to astrology from which the field did not begin to recover until the 1960s.

His mistake cast a long shadow. To this day, too many astrologers avoid mundane ingress charts—the type of chart that Carter used to justify his prediction. To some extent, this was Carter's doing, since his postwar book on mundane astrology, *An Introduction to Political Astrology*, insisted that ingress charts "have been weighed in the balance and found wanting."

It's a poor workman who blames his tools, however. The problem was not that ingress charts are inaccurate, it was that Carter read into the 1939 Aries ingress what he wanted to read there, and he ignored obvious signs that pointed in a direction that contradicted his personal preferences. This is a risk that mundane astrologers must always take into account. Most people who take up mundane astrology do it because they're interested in politics, and it's a very rare human being who can be interested in politics without taking sides. As Carter's example shows, it's crucial to be able to set your own enthusiasms aside when interpreting a mundane chart, or you'll risk making a fool of yourself the way he did.

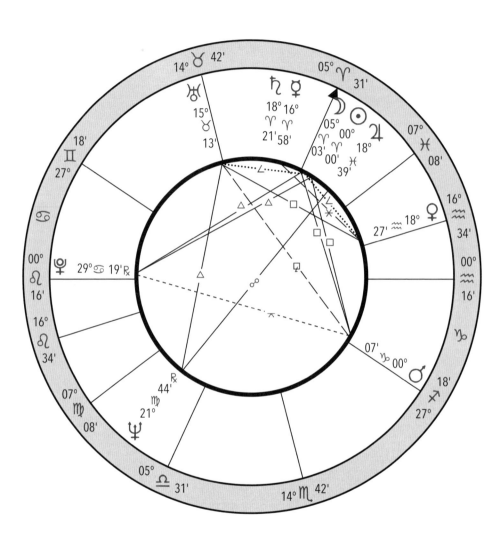

Aries 1939 ingress chart for London

You'll find the Aries 1939 ingress chart for London on p. 110. It's well worth comparing this to Carter's comments on this chart in *An Introduction to Political Astrology*. They run as follows:

"We find here an almost exact square of the Sun to Mars, which is assuredly appropriate to the year. Still, Sun is also trine Pluto. The Moon shares both contacts. It is not a good map, but under a belief in its predominant importance I announced at the Harrogate Convention that war was improbable; the Sun square Mars seemed to me rather indicative of the re-armament that was then under way. The position of Venus in the 8th sextile the ruler of that house and Mercury, though also square Uranus, appeared reassuring. Here was an example of faulty judgment much to be regretted, for it was widely reported in the northern press."

"Much to be regretted" indeed! Let's take a look at the chart with an eye toward what the standard mundane methods indicate.

The first thing to keep in mind—it is in fact one of the essential rules of traditional mundane astrology—is that house placements matter. An ingress chart covers the entire range of human activities for the period it rules, and its influences divide up neatly by house placement, modified by the traditional rulerships of the planets. The mistake of ignoring house placements and applying a planet to some subject it does not rule in the chart under consideration is a very common one and has been responsible for a great many bad predictions in mundane astrology.

This, to begin with, is why Carter's comment about Venus is irrelevant. The 8th house, where Venus is located, governs foreign trade and investment; it has nothing to do with peace or war. Venus is very slightly dignified by term in Aquarius, afflicted by a semisquare with the Moon and a square with Uranus and assisted by sextiles with Mercury and Saturn. This predicts that foreign trade and investment, otherwise fairly stable (the Moon and Saturn aspects), will be disrupted by a sudden change in conditions (the Uranus and Moon aspects). It says nothing about peace and only indirectly hints at war—the sudden change, of course, was the outbreak of the Second World War and the beginning of U-boat activity against British shipping, with submarine technology as a classic Uranus factor.

Pluto is a more significant figure in this chart. As noted in an earlier section, I don't use Pluto in my mundane charts, precisely because predictions based on Pluto positions and aspects are so often wrong, but this is a case where he communicates something worth noticing. On the cusp of the first house, trine Sun and Moon and inconjunct Mars, he announces major misjudgments affecting British life, which both the government and the people will survive, and from which both will ultimately benefit (Sun and Moon trine Pluto). His inconjunct with Mars—well, we'll discuss that when we get to the meaning of this chart's important Mars placement. Nothing in Pluto's placement in this chart predicts peace.

With these points dealt with, we can discuss those things in the chart that predict war—and there are several of them. Mars, the planet of war, is the most important of these. In this chart he squares both luminaries, a classic sign of war. The square with the Moon is the more important of the two because of her very close conjunction with the midheaven, which gives her and all her aspects much more power than usual. Here's what H. S. Green's *Mundane or National Astrology*, the standard English-language textbook on mundane astrology in Carter's time, has to say about the Moon in a hostile aspect with Mars: "If in an angle, foreign troubles, danger or war, or even actual war; very vexed questions arise and prove difficult of settlement."

Since the Sun in this chart is more than 5° from the midheaven, he is cadent, which weakens him, but his square with Mars still warns of serious trouble. Here's Green again: "Disputes, quarrels, and disagreements either at home or with other countries, and especially affecting the house occupied by Mars; a warlike feeling is aroused, waves of excitement are felt, party differences are widened." That plus the Moon-Mars square indicates serious international trouble and a real risk of war. The inconjunct between Mars and Pluto? Since the inconjunct is the aspect of frustration, that could be taken as a warning of the frustrating defeats and failures that beset the British military in the first months of the war. Since the inconjunct is a minor aspect, however, it does not outweigh the force of two close squares with the luminaries.

Carter's comment about rearmament shows how he missed the obvious meanings of these aspects. The 6th house is the house of the armed forces, and a well-dignified Mars in the 6th can indeed indicate a military buildup. Mars, however, is in very mixed dignity in this chart. He is exalted in Capricorn, but all his aspects are hostile: he is square the Sun and Moon, sesquisquare Uranus, and (if you use Pluto) inconjunct Pluto. Thus this chart predicts that Britain's armed forces were essentially strong and would undergo substantial rearmament but would also be battered by accidents and sudden reversals—and of course this is exactly how things turned out.

Let's move on. War with other countries belongs to the 7th house, and the ruler of the 7th is Uranus, who is in his fall in Taurus in the 11th house. His aspects are mostly negative—he is trine Neptune but semisquare the Moon, square Venus, and sesquisquare Mars—so on the whole, he is very poorly dignified. An afflicted Uranus ruling the 7th warns of serious problems and complications in foreign affairs, driven by enmity, rivalry, and disagreement. An afflicted Uranus located in the 11th warns that Parliament will do a very poor job of handling the resulting crisis, not least because Venus rules the 11th, the house of the legislative branch, and is square Uranus. Combined with the dire indications offered by Mars, this makes the risk of war more pronounced.

The trine linking Uranus and Neptune, by the way, also has a message to offer. In mundane astrology the 3rd house is, among other things, the house of neighboring countries, and in the international crisis predicted by this chart, Britain's most significant neighboring countries were its historic allies Belgium and France. Both remained firmly in the British camp when the crisis came—and both collapsed with astonishing speed once the Wehrmacht lunged west. This is shown by Neptune's poor condition in this chart. He is in his detriment in Virgo, retrograde, and afflicted by opposition with Jupiter in the 9th—this latter indicates the pacifist and defeatist sentiments that weakened both nations fatally. Jupiter opposite Neptune can also warn of treachery and double-dealing between nations, and of course that also played a significant role in the opening rounds of hostilities once war came.

Another very troubling placement in this chart is Saturn in the 10th house. This is one of the loudest warning sirens in astrology. In a natal chart, it predicts a sudden and final fall from a position of relative power; it appears in that role in the natal charts of Kaiser Wilhelm II, Adolf Hitler, and John F. Kennedy, for example. In mundane charts it has a similar meaning, warning of impending disaster in the political sphere. At the very least, it indicates that the government then in office is not long for this world. (Neville Chamberlain's government, then in power in Britain, just barely survived the end of the period governed by this chart, collapsing on May 10, 1940.) When reinforced by a severe essential debility, as in this case, it can mean the fall of an empire. (The British Empire, the largest empire in human history, was a walking corpse by the end of the Second World War and fell apart completely over the following decade.)

Yet, there's a further implication here, since Saturn is in Aries, which is ruled by Mars, and Mars is in Capricorn, which is ruled by Saturn. When two planets each appear in the sign the other rules, this is called mutual reception, and a simple rule governs the interpretation of planets in mutual reception: each one acts as though it were in the other's place, as well as in its own. Saturn in Capricorn in the 6th is a very fortunate sign for the British military and accurately predicts the extraordinary mobilization of the British economy that followed the declaration of war. On the other hand, Saturn square Sun and Saturn square Moon are both seriously baleful aspects, warning of severe difficulties facing the government and the people. With the Moon conjunct the midheaven, in particular, the latter aspect warns that whoever resides at Number 10 Downing Street should begin looking for new lodgings in the not-too-distant future.

Mars in Aries in the 10th, however, is the indication that matters most. An angular Mars in his own sign is a classic mundane sign of impending war. Unafflicted, he announces a war that Britain can win; conjunct Mercury, he foretells the immense role played by scientific innovation, communication, and espionage (all Mercury matters) in the war; his sextile with Venus in the

8th shows the equally immense role that economic support from the United States and British colonies overseas would play in helping Britain survive the war. One way or another, however, war was very clearly on its way.

I suspect that the mutual reception between Mars and Saturn in this chart predicts, among other things, the number of people who were taken by surprise just as C. E. O. Carter was by the outbreak of war. Mars acts as though he was angular in Aries, but he is not actually in that position; just as Saturn functions as though he was in Capricorn in the 6th even though he wasn't. The danger of war was thus invisible to politicians as well as astrologers, and war broke out as a result of fatal miscalculations on the part of German, British, and French politicians, all of whom assumed that the other side would back down, and were appalled to find out how wrong they were.

Equally, Hitler and his generals assumed that Britain would be a pushover once the Wehrmacht got to work, and discovered the hard way that they had misjudged their opponent. The suggestion that this was signaled by the mutual reception is a hypothesis and will require much more research to take it beyond that stage, but it will be worth examining mutual receptions in other mundane charts to see if the same theme of misperception and miscalculation appears there.

Even without this hypothesis, however, the 1939 Aries ingress for London was a very difficult chart predicting serious trouble in foreign policy and a significant risk of war. C. E. O. Carter was an otherwise capable astrologer, and he should have given adequate weight to the square between Mars and the luminaries, on the one hand, and the dismal condition of Uranus as ruler of the 7th house, on the other hand. There was, as it turns out, a reason why he did not do this, and it is a distinctly unpleasant reason. When German panzer divisions crossed the border into Poland on September 1, 1939, and started the Second World War, the issue of *Astrology* that was on British newsstands that day featured this comment by Carter in his quarterly editorial:

> Hence I remain very hopeful for peace. It is indeed deplorable that two nations near akin racially, as are the English and Germans, should be at loggerheads.

Those were not harmless words in 1939. They were, to be precise, words that were used over and over again by the pro-German faction in British public life in the years leading up to the Second World War. The reference to race is the giveaway here, since it was only the pro-German faction in Britain that echoed Nazi *Rassenlehre* in this way. Since that war, very few people have talked about the considerable size of that faction, or the extent to which pacifist movements in Britain and other Western countries before the war overlapped with groups in sympathy with "the new Germany," as Hitler's regime was called back then by its fans abroad.

Now of course this was before "blitzkrieg" and "Gestapo" became household words in most of the world's languages, before the Final Solution became a matter of public knowledge, when anti-Semitism was almost as socially acceptable in Britain and the United States as it was in Germany, and when people of goodwill could still manage to convince themselves that all the ugly rumors emanating from Germany were the work of pro-Soviet agitators. The fact remains that Carter allowed his political sympathies to cloud his mind and distract him from the clear indications of impending trouble in the ingress chart he was analyzing. Every student of mundane astrology should keep this in mind and put their political sympathies on the shelf while trying to make sense of a mundane chart.

Our second example relies on another famous misstep by C. E. O. Carter. I feel a little bad about having to pick on him again, but it can't be helped. Carter's insistence in *An Introduction to Political Astrology* that ingress charts were effectively useless as tools for the mundane astrologer played a significant role in distracting attention from classic mundane technique and thus made the task of the political and economic astrologer harder than it had to be. What's more, his mistakes are extremely educational. Studying the places where he went wrong is a great way to figure out what to avoid.

Carter presented two examples of ingress charts in the book just cited. One, which we've already examined, was the London Aries ingress chart for 1939; the other, which we'll examine now, is the London Aries ingress chart for 1914. Before we proceed with an analysis, I would encourage each reader to take a good long look at it before we proceed.

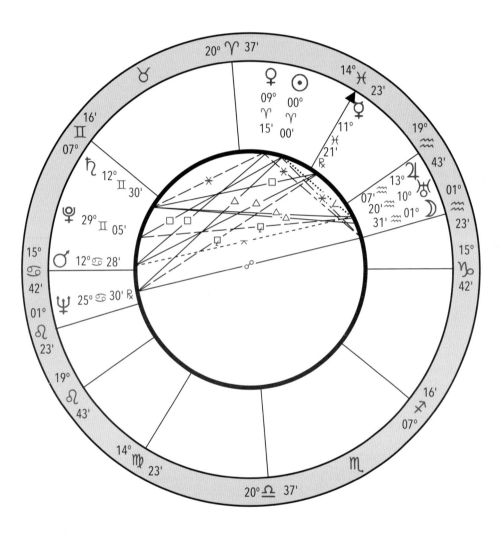

The London Aries ingress chart for 1914

This is what Carter says about it:

> It will be agreed, the writer believes, that this is hardly the figure that one would expect to herald the beginning of the era of ruthless war and political knavery and oppression that has actually been in full spate ever since August 1914. It is true that two malefics are near the ascendant (at least at London) and the ruler of the map is on cusp 8 (Placidus). Jupiter and Uranus are also in the 8th house, but they are sextile Venus and trine Saturn? The Sun itself is sextile Moon and quintile Saturn. It is also true that the Sun is in close square to Pluto, which was of course unknown at the time. [He then goes on to talk about details from the Berlin chart, which are irrelevant to our purpose.]

It will indeed be agreed by this writer that the chart Carter presents does not herald the beginning of an era of war, knavery, and oppression. That doesn't make it an inaccurate chart in this case. Ingress charts don't herald the arrival of eras—they describe political and economic conditions during periods of three, six, or twelve months, depending on the modality of the zodiacal sign rising at the moment of the ingress. That's what they do, and they do it very well, but it's all they do. Studying an ingress chart and expecting it for foretell the character of the following quarter century is a little like looking at an ordinary pocket watch and expecting it to show you the precession of the equinoxes.

With this in mind, take another look at the chart, and the more serious problem with Carter's analysis becomes instantly clear. You'll find that Cancer rises. Cancer is a cardinal sign, and ingress charts with cardinal signs rising apply for only three months—in this case, from March 21, 1914, to June 22, 1914. The assassination of Archduke Franz Ferdinand, the event that started the war, took place on June 28, 1914, and the combatant nations declared war on one another between July 28 and August 4. *The outbreak of the First World War did not happen during the period ruled by the Aries ingress chart.* Carter, in other words, missed one of the most basic details of classic mundane astrology, making the kind of mistake that beginners embarrass themselves by doing. It's a good thing he didn't have the chance to issue this prediction in the spring of 1914, or he would have had another world-class clunker to his credit.

With this in mind, what can we learn from studying the 1914 Aries ingress chart for London? Quite a bit, as it happens. The months immediately before the outbreak of war that year have gone down in history as a last golden moment before the world fell apart, and it's easy to see from this chart why that should have been so. At the same time, the stresses that were about to explode in one of the world's most disastrous wars can also be seen clearly in the chart. Let's take it a step at a time.

First of all, with Cancer rising, the Moon rules this chart. The Moon is in very mixed condition, peregrine in Aquarius, and gaining no help from her placement in a succedent house. She receives considerable benefit through a sextile with the Sun but a comparable share of trouble through an opposition with a retrograde Neptune in the 1st house. An afflicted Moon ruling the 1st, and in hostile aspect with a planet in the 1st, speaks of dissatisfaction with the existing political and economic order among the masses, and with Neptune as the afflicting planet, that dissatisfaction is being fed by a radical political movement (Neptune is the planet of idealism and radicalism). Of course that was very much the case in Britain in 1914, afflicted with a top-heavy class structure that drove the rise of the radical labor movement of the era.

For the period of this ingress, however, that dissatisfaction was not destined to find a release. This is seen by the Sun's position in the chart, strengthened by placement in the angular 10th house and by important favorable aspects. Notice how the Sun, in sextile aspect with the Moon and trine with Neptune, manages the strain between them in a way that benefits the established order of society and the government (Sun in the 10th house of political power). In Britain in 1914, that was in fact the way that politics worked; both the labor movement and the unorganized masses had been largely convinced that their best option was to work through existing political institutions, especially the Liberal Party.

Both these aspects are separating, however, and so they represent a state of affairs that had already passed its peak and would not last long—as of course it did not. The Labour Party, founded in 1900, was in the process of outflanking the Liberals from the Left and in 1922 would become one of the two dominant parties in British politics, driving the Liberals into permanent minority-party status. In the spring of 1914, however, that was still in the future. The working-class vote was still divided among the Liberal Party, the Labour Party, and the Independent Labour Party, and few people thought that the Liberal Party, one of the two main British parties since the party system itself emerged, was about to be shouldered aside. This chart doesn't show that act of displacement—an ingress chart shows only what will happen within the time frame it covers—but it shows the rising strains that would eventually make that happen.

There's plenty more that can be learned from this chart about the details of political and economic life in Britain in 1914, and I encourage readers to go through the chart house by house and see what they can figure out, then read a good book or two on Britain just before the war to see how well they did. (This sort of retrospective study is a very useful habit for students of mundane astrology, since there's no better way to learn what a current chart might be hinting at.) Since the point Carter tried and failed to make had to do with war, however, let's move on.

War in an ingress chart is primarily shown by the 7th house and its ruler, with the 10th house of politics and the 6th house of the military also important. Mars, as the planet of war, is also of crucial importance in any such analysis. We'll take these factors one at a time.

The 7th house in this chart has Capricorn on the cusp, and Saturn is therefore its ruler. Saturn in this chart is in his day triplicity in Gemini, which gives him some dignity, although he is weakened by placement in the cadent 12th house. More important in this case, however, is his aspects: he is trine his fellow outer planets Jupiter and Uranus, and sextile Venus, though he also suffers from a square with Mercury. The image of a period of stability, brittle in itself but propped up by powerful outside forces, fits the nature of the time very well.

Of those outside forces, one of the most important is indicated by Venus in the 10th house, who is not only sextile Saturn in the 12th but also sextile Jupiter and Uranus in the 8th. Venus in this chart represents the international pacifist movement, which was huge and influential in the decade or two immediately before the First World War. The movement was strongly supported by important figures in the British government (Venus in the 10th)—so long, that is, as it didn't interfere with Britain's military domination of its worldwide empire—and by institutions (12th house) and industries associated with foreign trade (8th house). As it turned out, huge though it was, the pacifist movement of those years had all the strength of puff pastry. The moment that war was declared, the vast majority of its supporters pivoted at once and backed the war effort. In the spring of 1914, however, nobody knew that yet.

The cluster of planets in the 8th house of this chart is another indicator that matters here. The 8th house is the house of international trade and finance, and in an ingress chart it rules such factors as imports, exports, investment to and from overseas markets, and the balance of trade. In the spring of 1914, Britain was the center of the world economy due to its huge empire, its control of maritime trade routes, its gargantuan industrial sector, and the status of the British pound sterling as the international reserve currency of the time. A very large share of British jobs in 1914 depended directly or indirectly on foreign trade (Moon in 8th), which made Britain much richer than it would otherwise be (Jupiter in 8th). Britain's dominance in international trade was far more vulnerable than it looked, however, since other countries—notably Germany and the United States—had already begun to take the lead in many emerging technologies (Uranus in and ruling 8th).

The stellium in the 8th thus helped reinforce the increasingly brittle peace of the time. Like the trine and sextile with the Sun that hold the Moon and Neptune in an unstable balance, however, both the trines that unite Jupiter and Uranus to Saturn are separating. Once again, a condition of relative stability and security is waning silently as we watch.

Another indication worth studying is given by Neptune. Pisces, the sign ruled by Neptune, is on the midheaven, influencing the behavior of government, and Neptune himself, as already noted, is retrograde in the first house. Not only is Neptune retrograde in this chart, but he is opposite the Moon and sesquisquare Mercury; on the flip side, he is angular and trine the Sun, which are powerful dignities. A well-dignified Neptune represents idealism, an ill-dignified one deception and delusion. It's clear from this chart that both these factors had a major impact on the British government—and that both of them were driven at least in part by a desire on the part of politicians to play to the idealism and the delusions of the electorate (Neptune in 1st).

Mars, as already noted, is a crucial planet in any mundane chart in which war might be an issue. In this chart, Mars is in very weak shape: he is in his fall in Cancer, in the cadent 12th house, square Venus and inconjunct Jupiter, though he receives some help from a trine with Mercury. With a well-dignified Saturn ruling the 7th and Mars in so weak a position, it's quite clear that war was very unlikely to break out during the spring of 1914, and of course war did not break out that spring (conditions were very different once the Cancer ingress took effect at the beginning of summer). Yet, there are two Martian factors in the Aries ingress chart that whisper a warning.

The first is Mars's placement, in the 12th but conjunct the Ascendant. Planets that conjoin the angles from the cadent side seem to be associated with unexpected crises and misjudgments—the afflicted Moon in the London Aries ingress in 1939, conjunct the midheaven from the 9th house side, is another good example. This suggests to me that while the risk of war was very low while the ingress lasted, the shadow of war was already beginning to creep over Britain as a conflict further out came closer.

The second is the aforementioned trine with Mercury. Mercury is in his fall in Pisces, retrograde, and weakly placed in the cadent 9th house; he is square Saturn and sesquisquare Neptune, the ruler of Pisces—and he is also conjunct the midheaven from the 9th-house side, another indicator of misjudgment and of a failure to recognize impending crises. What the Mercury placement in this chart suggests is that the British government in 1914 had either drastically misjudged the situation in Europe or had failed to communicate its intentions clearly to other nations—or both. Accounts of the crisis that burst over Europe shortly after this ingress passed off suggest that in fact both of these were the case.

A final factor of interest in this chart has to do with Pluto. As already noted, I avoid using Pluto in my mundane charts, since relying on Plutonian influences has proven to be so effective a way to make inaccurate predictions; the 1939 ingress chart, in which Carter let a favorable aspect between the Sun and Pluto distract him from serious indications of a major crisis in international relations, is another example of this. This chart is another; Pluto and the Sun are in a close square, which in modern astrological theory is a sign of dire consequences—yet, the spring of 1914 was a quiet, golden season without massive trouble.

At the same time, Pluto-Sun aspects may sometimes indicate hidden but real problems. In the Cancer 1914 ingress chart, the Sun and Pluto are almost exactly conjunct, with only 37 minutes of arc between them, another dire sign—and that summer, Europe blew sky high. What this suggests to me is that the astrology of Pluto may not be as well understood as the dwarf planet's more enthusiastic partisans think. Since astrology is an empirical science, it may take another century or so of ingress charts and other explorations in mundane astrology to figure out exactly how to make accurate predictions by using Pluto.

Given the current state of the art in mundane astrology, this chart offers a very useful glance at how to read an ingress chart—and how not to do so. An ingress chart, as this shows, does not herald the beginning of an era; it simply provides a snapshot of conditions in a particular country for a particular period of three, six, or twelve months. You can't use it to foretell conditions after that period is up. Keep that in mind, and you'll be much less likely to make a fool of yourself the way that C. E. O. Carter did.

CASE STUDY 2

BULLETS AT THE FAIR

There's a certain amount of controversy over retrospective analysis of astrological charts. Some astrologers, including some very good ones, insist that it's a waste of time to go over a chart with 20/20 hindsight and pick out the indications for events that have already happened. I understand their logic, but I disagree with it. Where mundane astrology is concerned, we're still in the process of recovering a largely forgotten tradition and retooling it for the changed conditions of the modern world. The indications displayed by past charts, compared to the events that they heralded, are important guides in that work of revival. That's why I went back over C. E. O. Carter's disastrously bad mundane analyses in the previous case study, and why I am examining more historical events in this and the following case study, with an eye toward learning what we can from the relevant charts.

For this case study, I set out to find a dramatic, well-documented event in the last century or two of political history that could be discussed calmly, even in the current overheated climate of opinion. That might seem like a tall order, except that so few people these days know or care about things that happened before they were born. You'll have to hunt long and hard to find anyone who gets bent out of shape about the great political events of the turn of the last century, for example. With that in mind, let's turn back the pages to one of the most shocking US news stories of 1901: the assassination of President William McKinley by anarchist Leon Czolgosz at the Pan-American Exposition in Buffalo on September 6, 1901.

Some background is in order. McKinley was a Republican who served in Congress and as governor of Ohio before he reached the White House. He won the bitterly contested election of 1896 against Democrat William Jennings Bryan on a platform of a stable gold-backed currency and steep tariffs to protect American jobs against foreign competition.

His first term saw the US recover from the depression of 1896 and achieve rapid economic growth. Under his leadership, the US also took its first steps toward overseas empire with the annexation of Hawaii and the seizure of Puerto Rico, Guam, and the Philippines in the Spanish-American War of 1898. These steps were unpopular with the intelligentsia and some of the political class but very popular with the electorate, and he won reelection in 1900 by a landslide.

In 1901, meanwhile, anarchism was the most popular flavor of radical politics on the American Far Left. Leon Czolgosz was a typical recruit, a factory worker who had been left destitute by one of the many financial panics of late-nineteenth-century America, and he had embraced the frankly crackbrained anarchist theory of "attentat"—the notion that the murder of prominent political figures would win publicity and sympathy for anarchism. After taking in a speech by anarchist celebrity Emma Goldman in Cleveland, Czolgosz went to Buffalo intending to shoot the president. Presidential security was lax in those days, and he was able to get close enough to shoot McKinley twice with a pistol. The president lingered for a week and then died.

The attentat was a catastrophe for anarchism in the US. It never again reached the level of popularity it had before that September day, since most Americans thereafter associated it with the pointless murder of a popular president. The nation went through one of its typical spasms of mass grieving and then rallied around Theodore Roosevelt, McKinley's vice president, who was already nearly as popular as McKinley had been and who went on to become one of the most charismatic presidents in US history (there's good reason why his face is on Mt. Rushmore). The stock market suffered a brief plunge but recovered promptly, and the US continued the long trajectory of economic expansion punctuated by sharp financial panics, which ended only with the coming of the Great Depression.

Those are the events to keep in mind as we proceed to consider two charts. The first is the chart for McKinley's second inauguration in Washington, DC, at noon on March 4, 1901. The second is the ingress chart for the United States that was in effect at the time of his assassination, the Washington, DC, Cancer ingress, 10:27 p.m. on June 21, 1901. We'll take them one at a time.

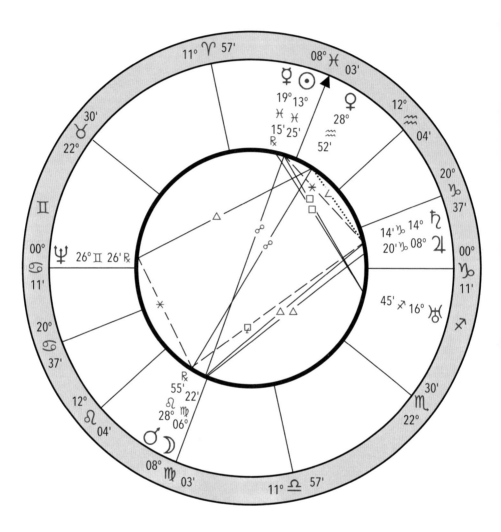

The chart for President William McKinley's second inauguration in
Washington, DC, at noon on March 4, 1901

Until 1932, presidential inaugurations in the US were always on March 4, unless that was a Sunday, at or around noon. It was a good astrological time: the Sun was always conjunct midheaven and in Pisces, where he is peregrine and thus relatively weak without being any more forcefully debilitated. (Since the date was changed, he's been in its detriment in Aquarius, which helps explain our nation's political trajectory since then.) Since its sign and house are fixed by statute, the only things you can read from the Sun's position in any individual inauguration chart are (1) the aspects affecting it and (2) the condition of the ruler of the house in which it is placed.

The aspects influencing the Sun in this chart are an opposition with the Moon, a conjunction with Mercury, a sextile with Saturn, and a square with Uranus. The Moon in this chart is in weak condition, peregrine in Virgo, placed in the cadent 3rd house and afflicted by a conjunction with Mars as well as the opposition with the Sun; this signifies the ineffective opposition that McKinley faced from sectors of the political classes who were opposed to imperialism and to his economic policies. Mercury is, if anything, weaker, being in his fall in Pisces, retrograde, combust, and afflicted by a square with Uranus, though he recovers a little strength by his placement in an angular house. He represents the intellectuals and mass media of the time who were aligned with McKinley and said pretty much whatever the party bosses told them to say.

The sextile with Saturn is a more significant factor. Saturn in this chart is in his rulership in Capricorn, angular, conjunct the benefic planet Jupiter, trine the Moon, and sextile the Sun—it's hard to think of any way he could be in better condition, and his sextile with the Sun is close, less than a degree from perfection. In this chart he gives the McKinley administration and the country a great deal of political stability, especially in foreign affairs (Saturn in the 7th house). Saturn and Jupiter were approaching one of their great conjunctions in this chart and would perfect that conjunction on November 28, 1901, marking a significant shift in US politics that would endure until 1921.

The square with Uranus is more revealing. Uranus in this chart is peregrine in Sagittarius in the cadent 6th house, and Sagittarius is intercepted in that house. Sun square Uranus is a warning of sudden and unexpected crisis. In the 6th, it suggests that McKinley's health might be at risk, but it gives no obvious warning that the crisis would be brought about by an assassin's bullet.

One further indication is worth examining here. Neptune, the planet of mass movements and dreams of a better future, is in the 12th house, conjunct the ascendant. He is in his exaltation in Gemini, but retrograde. Here he can be seen as the significator of the anarchist movement, which at that moment had no particular connection with McKinley—Neptune is not in aspect with the Sun—and relates mostly to the opposition between Mars in the 3rd and Venus in the 9th: that is, the conflict between the anarchist movement's dreams of universal justice and its odd habit of trying to communicate those dreams by violent acts (the 3rd is the house of communications and media). Overall, it is clear from this reading that some kind of health crisis waits for McKinley, and that anarchism would have a significant influence on his term, but the details cannot be determined from the inauguration chart.

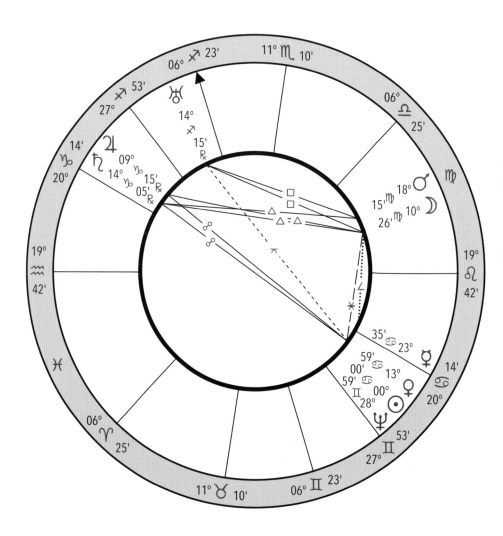

The ingress chart for the United States at assassination of President William McKinley, the Washington, DC, Cancer ingress at 10:27 p.m. on June 21, 1901

The ingress chart is another matter. In this second chart, Aquarius rises, and so the chart governed US politics and society from the date of the ingress until the next Aries ingress in March 1902. Aquarius is ruled by Uranus, who is angular in the 10th house, though still peregrine and retrograde to boot; he is also square the Moon and Mars and inconjunct Venus, making him an extremely baleful indication. From this chart it is clear that some kind of sudden shock will affect the nation. Mars square Uranus is a particularly negative indication, being associated with political violence and, if other testimonies support this, the death of a leading politician. Mars is strongly placed in the angular 7th house, dignified by mixed triplicity with Virgo and supported by a conjunction with the Moon and a trine with strongly dignified Saturn. Mars is, however, intercepted, and so the act defined by the Mars-Uranus square is limited in its scope and effect.

Now look at the Sun, the significator of President McKinley. He is in the fifth house, which rules fairs and expositions as well as all other places of amusement, and his only aspect is a close conjunction with Neptune. Other than that, he's all by himself. Neptune has a very bad reputation in the nineteenth-century astrological texts where I learned most of my mundane astrology. Those texts generally treat him as a tremendously malefic planet in political matters, and when I first started dabbling in mundane astrology, I put that down to the political prejudices of the authors and treated him as a benefic, as he's always been in my personal progression and transit charts. A study of McKinley's fate was one of the things that made me change my mind.

A hostile aspect between the Sun and Neptune is the most negative of all aspects in traditional mundane astrology: "Something in the nature of a downfall or collapse takes place," says H. S. Green. I've seen that happen repeatedly with squares and oppositions in mundane charts for past events. Now here we have a Sun-Neptune conjunction having exactly the same indication. One of the distinctive features of a malefic planet is that a conjunction with him is a hostile aspect—and in this chart, certainly, Neptune functions as a malefic. The significator of the president comes into conjunction with the planet of anarchism and popular unrest, and something in the nature of a downfall or collapse did indeed take place. This is the kind of thing that can be learned from retrospective analysis of charts, and I've altered my own take on Neptune as a result.

Note, however, that it affected only McKinley and the mood of the public—and Czolgosz, of course, who narrowly escaped being torn to pieces by a furious mob at the scene of the crime and was promptly tried, convicted, and sent to the electric chair after McKinley's death. The politically active classes rallied around the government—this is shown by the trine between the Moon and Jupiter, which rules the 10th house of the executive branch and the 11th house of Congress—and the radicalism of the nineteenth century's last years gave way to a renewed conservatism and a fixation on stability at all costs—this is shown by the trine between the Moon and Saturn, the conjunction between Jupiter and Saturn, Saturn's rulership of the sign in which Jupiter is placed, Saturn's rulership of the 12th house of institutions, and also the fact that both Jupiter and Saturn are retrograde in the 11th house of legislation in this chart.

Meanwhile, anarchism's day in the United States was rapidly drawing to a close. For more than a decade before Czolgosz pulled the trigger and got himself his fifteen minutes of infamy, Neptune, the planet of anarchism and political radicalism generally, had been in his exaltation in Gemini. In this chart, he is only a degree from the end of that sign, and the sign he rules, Pisces, was intercepted in the 1st house, suggesting the anarchist movement's transformation into an isolated subculture—a transformation that duly followed.

In this case, certainly, the ingress chart has shown itself to be a much more exact indication of events to come than the inauguration chart. The events that took place while both charts were in effect can be traced in either one, but the indications of the inauguration chart are considerably more general and less useful. I have found this to be generally true, and it helps explain why the ingress chart had its traditional reputation as the workhorse of mundane astrology.

CASE STUDY 3

THE UNCROWNED
KING

Another worthwhile case study, far enough in the past that most people can consider it without political passions getting in the way, focuses on one of the most shocking events of 1936: the abdication of Britain's uncrowned King Edward VIII. Some backstory may be useful here as well. Edward VIII was the eldest son of George V and thus by law and tradition the next heir to the British throne. Born in 1894, he earned a reputation as a fashionable playboy and womanizer, with a notable fondness for other men's wives. A scandal over a French sex worker, to whom Edward wrote a series of embarrassing letters, was narrowly averted in 1923 by frantic efforts on the part of British officials. After a series of other affairs, he met and became infatuated with Wallis Simpson, an American who was already on her second husband. The two of them quickly became the subject of lurid rumors.

Late on the night of January 20, 1936, George V died, and Edward was formally proclaimed king two days later. His behavior led many people in the British establishment to fear that he would fail to take his duties seriously and refuse to abide by the strict constitutional limits on royal involvement in politics. Meanwhile, Wallis Simpson filed for divorce, and Edward made it clear that he intended to marry her.

The prime minister, Stanley Baldwin, opposed the marriage; so did his cabinet, and so did the governments of the British Empire's other dominions, which had a say in the matter under the laws then in effect. So did the archbishop of Canterbury, the amusingly named Cosmo Lang, whose office gave him considerably more power in those days than his successor has today. Faced with a choice between the crown and the woman he loved,

Edward abdicated on December 10, and his brother took the throne as George VI.

The new king promptly made Edward a royal duke, a move that barred him from getting involved in British politics for the rest of his life, and ordered him to leave the country and not return unless he was invited; needless to say, the invitation never came. The Duke of Windsor, as he then became, married Wallis Simpson in France in 1937, spent the Second World War in exile as British governor of the Bahamas, and returned to France once the war was over. He died there in 1972.

From the perspective of mundane astrology, two charts govern the abdication of Edward VIII. The first is the chart for his formal public proclamation as king, at 10:00 a.m. on January 22, 1936, in London. The second is the ingress chart in effect at the time of his abdication: the Libra ingress for the United Kingdom at 5:25 a.m. on September 23, 1936, also in London. The first of these provides an overall view of his short reign—it would have been replaced by his coronation chart if he had been crowned—and the second shows the political climate in effect when the controversy over his intended marriage reached critical mass. As with the previous case study, we'll examine them one at a time.

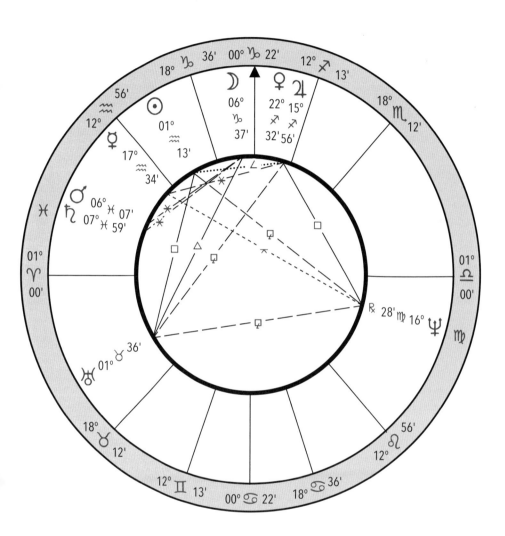

The chart for the formal public proclamation of King Edward VIII, at
10:00 a.m. on January 22, 1936, in London

The proclamation chart features a very interesting pattern of aspects, one that as far as I know hasn't been discussed yet in astrological literature. Aspect patterns form a fascinating field of astrological research, a branch of study that emerged in the twentieth century and has only just begun to be applied to mundane charts. Among the best-known patterns are the grand trine, which is formed by a triangle of three planets, each 120° from the other two, and the grand cross, which is formed by two pairs of opposed planets, 90° from each other. A grand trine, as the name suggests, is like a trine on rocket fuel, a very positive and benevolent pattern; the grand cross combines two oppositions and four squares into a potentially explosive pattern held in balance by tremendous tension.

You can see the pattern I have in mind in the chart, drawn by the aspects connecting the Sun, Jupiter, Uranus, and Neptune. The Sun and Uranus are square, Jupiter and Neptune are square, the Sun and Jupiter are semisquare, and the three pairs Sun-Neptune, Jupiter-Uranus, and Uranus-Neptune all are sesquisquare (all these aspects are very close, by the way, and all but one is applying, giving them additional strength). Since this pattern apparently hasn't been explored by other astrologers, I'll take the liberty of giving it a name: the wastebasket.

A wastebasket is like a lower-intensity grand cross. Where the grand cross is made up of two oppositions and four squares and thus embodies the two major hostile aspects, the wastebasket is made up of two squares, a semisquare, and three sesquisquares and so combines one major hostile aspect and two minor ones. A grand cross in mundane astrology always warns of major crises, challenges, and frustrations in national life, though it can also show strength and determination in the national mood, sufficient to meet these problems. A wastebasket, by comparison, suggests an abundance of minor crises, challenges, and frustrations in national life, which could be overcome if only there was enough strength and determination to do so.

Let's look a little more closely at the four planets that define the wastebasket. The Sun in this chart is in his fall in Aquarius, and all his aspects are hostile ones—not a good omen for the beginning of a king's reign! In a royal chart such as this one, the Sun afflicted in the 11th house warns of conflict between king and Parliament and predicts legal difficulties in the way of the king. It can indicate disorganization in government and the failure of proposed measures. Semisquare Jupiter, he predicts trouble over religious issues; square Uranus, he warns of serious trouble for the government and the monarch, caused by injudicious or unpopular actions; sesquisquare Neptune, he announces disorder and confusion and suggests that a downfall of some kind may be imminent.

Jupiter in this chart, by contrast, is in his rulership in Sagittarius, and he has two helpful aspects—a sextile with Mercury and a loose conjunction with Venus—giving him additional strength. He is, however, in a cadent house, which weakens him somewhat, and the hostile aspects from the other planets in the wastebasket pattern do the same. Jupiter in relatively good dignity in the 9th house gives strength to the laws and the legal system and also empowers the Church of England—Archbishop Lang's role in the abdication crisis is worth remembering here. Jupiter sesquisquare Uranus raises religious difficulties in Parliament, brings trouble for any new venture, and is unfortunate for the ruling power in any context. Jupiter square Neptune signals confusion and misunderstanding and guarantees hard feelings and mutual recriminations.

Uranus in this chart is a little less badly placed than the Sun but is still afflicted. He is in his fall in Taurus and is afflicted by hostile aspects with the Sun, Jupiter, and Neptune, but he receives support from a trine with the Moon, and he is also placed in the angular 1st house, which strengthens him. Uranus in the 1st, in bad but not extremely bad condition, warns of trouble, popular dissatisfaction, turbulence, and misfortunes for the government. Uranus sesquisquare Neptune brings on political trouble, discord, and delay and tends to predict that the head of state or head of government whose career it inaugurates will not hold office for a long time.

Neptune, finally, is in his detriment in Virgo, retrograde, and in the cadent 6th house and is afflicted by hostile aspects with four planets—in addition to the rest of the wastebasket, he is in an inconjunct aspect with Mercury! Though most planets in this chart are in bad condition, Neptune takes the prize for worst in show. A badly afflicted Neptune is the worst of all indications for a mundane chart, promising a disordered and unstable state of affairs ending in downfall. Added to the other indications in this chart, he promises a very difficult reign. Had Edward VIII been crowned, he could have had an astrologer elect a time and date for the coronation to bring good fortune to his reign, as John Dee did for Elizabeth I—but that never happened.

Let's glance at some of the other indications of the chart. Aries rises in this chart, and so Mars is the chart ruler. Having a malefic ruling the ascendant is not a welcome sign, especially when the planet in question is peregrine, intercepted, in a cadent house, and conjunct another malefic planet—and Mars is all of these things. He is not completely without dignity, being in sextile aspect with the Moon, but that is his only source of strength. All this is quite appropriate: in 1936, Britain was in the depths of the Great Depression, battered, impoverished, and increasingly menaced by the rising power of Nazi Germany.

The midheaven, which represents the government in power, is not much more promising. Capricorn is on the midheaven and so Saturn rules the government; there he is, right next to Mars in the 12th house. Saturn is dignified by face in the first 10 degrees of Pisces, so he has some essential dignity, and he also has the support of a sextile with the Moon, but he is intercepted, in a cadent house, and conjunct malefic Mars. As this suggests, Stanley Baldwin has not gone down in British history as one of the nation's strong and successful prime ministers. These days he is remembered mostly for having imitated the grand old Duke of York in the song, by presiding over disarmament in the first half of his time in office and rearmament in the second half.

Weak as Baldwin's government is shown to be in this chart, it has several crucial strengths. The first is shown by the Moon in the 10th house. She is in her detriment in Capricorn but receives considerable help from placement in the angular 10th and from helpful aspects with all three of the malefic planets—sextiles with Mars and Saturn and a trine with Uranus. Since the Moon is the significator of the political classes, this shows that Baldwin's government could count on the support of Britain's elites in dealing with the new king. The second strength is shown by Capricorn also ruling the 11th house: Baldwin's government did not have to worry about losing control of Parliament in the event of trouble.

The third, and in many ways the most crucial, is on the other side of the chart: Cancer rules the cusps of the 4th house of the countryside and the 5th house of the wealthy. During this period, at least, the political classes could count on the support of ordinary Britons and the wealthy classes alike. This is reinforced by the conjunction between Mars, the ruler of the first house of the populace, and Saturn, the ruler of the 10th and 11th houses: the government and Parliament could count on the support of the masses if crisis came.

Note also the 7th-house cusp, which in this context represents Wallis Simpson, the woman Edward chose to marry. Its ruler is Venus, who is peregrine in Sagittarius in the cadent 9th house, representing her involvement in legal affairs (i.e., her divorce), and is not in aspect to any other planet. On the one hand, this indicates the simple reality that no one but Edward VIII thought that Simpson was a suitable choice as queen of Britain; on the other hand, it suggests that there may well have been much more going on in the succession crisis than a dispute over Mrs. Simpson. From her position in the chart, she simply wasn't that important—or perhaps the chart is saying that she didn't need to become a major obstacle to Edward's kingship.

A competent astrologer, looking over this chart, could have given Edward VIII good advice. If he had been prepared to bide his time, let his relationship with Wallis Simpson remain informal for the time being, and watch his step so as to avoid uniting the political class against him, he could have survived the critical first year or so of his reign and scheduled his coronation for a time and date that would have brought much more favorable influences to bear on the rest of his time on the throne. Apparently he didn't think to consult an astrologer, however, and the flurry of minor crises indicated by the wastebasket aspect pattern reached critical mass and overwhelmed him.

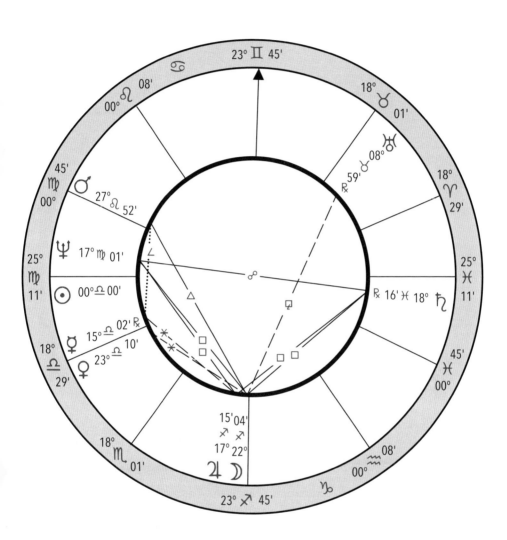

The Libra ingress chart at the time of King Edward VIII's abdication for the United Kingdom at 5:25 a.m. on September 23, 1936, in London

The crisis came under the 1936 Libra ingress chart. This is dominated by a more common and familiar aspect pattern: the T square, formed by an opposition between two planets with a third square to both. In this case, the third position is occupied by two planets, the Moon and Jupiter. A T square is three-quarters of a grand cross, and like a grand cross, it shows tensions rising to the breaking point. Unlike the grand cross, however, those tensions have an outlet, which is marked by the missing corner of the square. In this case, the outlet is in the 9th house, conjunct the midheaven: a legal action affecting the summit of the political system. That action turned out to be Edward VIII's abdication.

The specific tensions are clearly shown in the chart. Neptune rules the 7th house of marriage and indicates Mrs. Simpson. Saturn represents the religious and social conservatism that Edward's choice of bride had offended. The balance of power in the T square is held by the Moon, symbol of the political class, and Jupiter, symbol of the church and the laws—and these are in the 3rd house, which is, among other things, the house of siblings. Edward VIII had a brother, the future George VI, who was far more conventional in his habits and far more acceptable to the political classes. Furthermore, he had already provided the country with an heir, a charming and popular princess whom the royal family called Lillibet and the rest of us know as the late Queen Elizabeth II.

It's only fair to point out that the crisis could have been much worse than it was. All four of the planets that create it—the Moon, Jupiter, Saturn, and Neptune—are in cadent houses, and thus weakened. Both the Moon and Saturn are peregrine, and Neptune is in his detriment in Virgo; only Jupiter, comfortably placed in his rulership in Sagittarius, has any innate dignity at all. Again, there is nothing at work in the crisis that a modest amount of courage and determination could not have brushed aside, but these weren't available.

The Sun, the king's significator, is not directly affected by the T square, or by any other planet in the chart. He is conjunct the ascendant and thus relatively strong, but he is isolated from the action, as the former king was by the time this ingress chart finished its period of effect. Mercury, ruling the 10th house of government, is also in the angular 1st house, and he is dignified by night triplicity and strengthened by a sextile with Jupiter. The political classes had no independent power of action—the Moon's rulership in Cancer is intercepted in the 10th—but Baldwin was entirely able to apply pressure on their behalf. So the crisis came, and Edward crumpled under pressure and fled to France. Once there, he besieged his brother with so many demands for money that George VI finally ordered his staff to stop putting the calls through.

There were many more events in process in 1936, of course, and the ingress chart shows many of them. Britain in that year was facing an increasingly hostile world, as the brittle peace that followed the First World War broke apart at the seams, and the cumbersome machinery of the League of Nations proved hopelessly inadequate to deal with the rising strains; the domestic pressures that would bring drastic social change after the war were already evident as well. All this would take us far afield from the current subject, however.

The final point worth making here is that once again, Edward VIII could have benefited from competent astrological advice. Since the Sun was in the first house, conjunct the ascendant and not in aspect to any other planet, he could have distanced himself from the fracas and had his allies in Parliament negotiate some sort of compromise—for example, a morganatic marriage with Mrs. Simpson, one in which she would not become the queen and any children they had would not inherit the throne—or simply have left the issue of the marriage open until his position was more secure. Instead, he spent the rest of his life in exile, and English schoolchildren, putting new words to an old Christmas carol, sang, "Hark, the herald angels sing, Mrs. Simpson pinched our king." The wastebasket pattern turned out to be an accurate prediction of where Edward would end up.

CASE STUDY 4

———————————————————————————————

THE US FOUNDATION CHART

Foundation charts—charts cast for the founding of a political entity, such as a nation or a city—are not especially central to the classic tool kit of the mundane astrologer, but they do play a role in the art. As discussed earlier, they serve much the same function as the natal chart of a person and can be used in many of the same ways, provided that you can get an accurate date and time. That, of course, is very often the problem.

Standard practice in mundane astrology is to take the date, time, and place at which the current political entity was formally established as the data for the foundation chart, and in the case of countries that have undergone major political transformations in the last century or so, this allows for accurate charting. Thus, for example, there's no question what date, time, and place to use for Russia in current charts: it's a matter of public record that the Russian Federation was formally established at 5:19 p.m. local time, December 25, 1991, in Moscow. On the other end of the spectrum is the kingdom of England, which despite many alterations still has the monarchy established in 1066 after the Norman Conquest; the coronation of William I in London sometime around noon on December 25, 1066, is one potential date and time for England's foundation chart, but there's a lot of wiggle room and many alternative dates and times.

The United States falls into the space between these extremes. Most astrologers consider the foundation of the US to have taken place on July 4, 1776, in Philadelphia, when the Declaration of Independence was voted into effect by the Continental Congress. The big question is the time. If anybody wrote down the exact time, the document hasn't survived, but there are indications in surviving records. The memoirs of John Adams, Elbridge Gerry,

John Hancock, and Thomas Jefferson, all of whom were present, mention that the vote was held after a day of debate, in the late afternoon or early evening. Celebrations in Philadelphia in the years immediately following independence are known to have started around five o'clock in the afternoon.

Then there's the most complicated source of the lot, the horoscope published in astrologer Ebenezer Sibly's 1780 book *The Celestial Science of Astrology*. Sibly, like many intellectuals in England at that time, was a fervent supporter of the American Revolution, and he included details of the 1776 ingress charts for England and America in the section of his book on mundane charts. He also included a supposed chart for American independence—but it's an impossible chart. The house cusps and lunar position he gives did not appear together in any place on Earth on the day in question. The problems aren't subtle ones. Anyone who knew enough about astrology to check Sibly's work would have known in a matter of minutes that the chart was bogus. The question is why Sibly put so bizarrely wrong a chart into his book.

Mundane astrologer Ed Kohout, in a fine four-part online essay, has sketched the complex landscape of political intrigue and astrological knowledge that lies behind the Sibly chart. The very short form is that the Sibly chart is encoded. Its house cusps are taken from the London ingress chart then in effect, while the planetary positions are taken from the actual Philadelphia chart. The time given—10:10 p.m.—is the local time in London that corresponds to the time in Philadelphia. Decode the Sibly chart and you get the contemporaneous astrological data for the signing of the Declaration of Independence: 5:10 p.m. local time, July 4, 1776.

Why was it encoded? We'll get to that in a moment. The thing I'd like to note first is that the habit of concealment didn't go away once the United States won its independence. During much of the twentieth century, the most common foundation chart for the United States presented in books on astrology used the time of 2:17 a.m. on July 4. Not one scrap of evidence backs the claim that the Declaration was voted into effect at two o'clock in the morning, when by all accounts most of the delegates were asleep in their beds, and the day of debate that culminated in the vote hadn't even happened yet. Nor, as far as I know, did anyone who circulated this chart try to justify its really odd choice of time.

A galaxy of other times have been proposed, ranging from the early morning until late at night on the fourth, and a range of other dates have also been suggested, beginning with July 2, 1776, and going from there to the first inauguration of George Washington on April 30, 1789. Some of this is the normal process of scholarly debate in the astrological community, but it seems very odd that the contemporaneous evidence for a time around 5:00 p.m. should have been so systematically ignored by so many astrologers for so long.

There is, as it happens, a reason for the secrecy—or rather, two reasons. The first is that the science of astrology in 1776 was still very close to its medieval roots. In Britain and the colonies alike, many of the people who practiced it knew that an accurate foundation chart could be used to predict the weaknesses and vulnerable times of a political entity. Since manuscript copies of books of astrological magic were still in circulation at that time, some may have known of the ways given in such volumes to curse a city or a nation, provided that certain details in its foundation chart were known. Many practitioners of astrological magic today go out of their way not to mention the complete data for their birth chart in public; in the same way, the data for the foundation chart of the United States may well have seemed worth concealing.

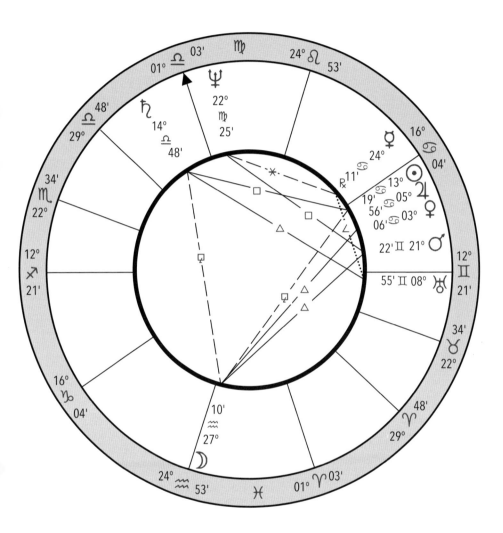

The foundation chart for American independence on July 4, 1776, around
5:10 p.m. local time in Philadelphia

Yet, there's another reason for secrecy, and it stands out like a flashing red light once you cast the chart for the time Sibly gives, shown on the previous page. On the whole, it's a favorable chart, and we'll discuss how that works out and what it predicts about the history of the United States in a moment. Yet, there's one detail that stands out to anyone who studies the predictive dimensions of astrology: Saturn is in the 10th house.

Saturn in the 10th is one of the most legendary placements in astrology. In natal charts, it has a very specific meaning: the person who has this placement in their chart will rise to great heights and then suddenly be flung down from them. As noted in an earlier case study, Kaiser Wilhelm II, Adolf Hitler, and John F. Kennedy all had Saturn in the 10th. In mundane charts, it has a similar signification. A political entity founded with Saturn in the 10th can expect to rise to great power and prominence and then meet a sudden disastrous end. It's understandable that American astrologers would want to avoid mentioning this!

Several caveats are worth mentioning here. The first is that it's impossible to know from the foundation chart when the sudden end will take place. That's true of natal charts too, as it happens: you can use progressions or solar returns (two standard ways of prediction using the natal chart) to tell when a sudden downfall is likely to happen, but—well, as the old saying goes, the stars incline, they do not compel. If Ebenezer Sibly had taken the chart shown here, for example, and progressed the Sun using the state-of-the-art methods of 1776, he would have known at a glance that the United States would face a potentially terminal crisis in the 1860s; that's when the Sun, progressed at a rate of 1 degree per year, would be applying to a conjunction with Saturn's placement. He would have been right, too, but the United States survived the Civil War era.

The second thing worth noting is that Saturn is fairly well dignified in this chart. He's in his exaltation in Libra, strengthened by placement in the angular 10th house and supported by a trine with Uranus, which was about to be discovered as Sibly published his book (it was first spotted by William Herschel in 1781). Admittedly, he is afflicted by both of the luminaries—an applying square with the Sun and an applying sesquisquare with the Moon—but plenty of charts with a dangerously placed Saturn are much, much worse. Thus the sudden end of the United States, whenever that happens, may be on the less traumatic end of collapse: something like the sudden implosion of the Soviet Union, for example, rather than nuclear holocaust or the like.

With that detail in mind, let's take a look at the foundation chart for the United States and see what else it has to tell us, using the standard tools of mundane astrology.

As with any other mundane chart, the planet ruling the ascendant also rules the chart as a whole. With Sagittarius rising, Jupiter rules this chart, and Jupiter is well placed: in his exaltation in Cancer, in the angular 7th house, and conjunct the lesser benefic Venus. He is, however, combust, being a little over 7 degrees from a separating conjunction with the Sun. A nation whose founding is ruled by a well-dignified Jupiter is destined to become very prosperous, to benefit substantially from foreign trade, and to experience fewer wars on its own territory than most countries do.

Placed in the 7th house, Jupiter predicts strong alliances with foreign countries and successful foreign relations generally. Venus conjunct Jupiter reinforces these indications and also suggests that it is a country where women will be unusually successful and prosperous, as compared to other nations. The conjunction between the Sun and Jupiter, however, predicts that lawsuits will be a popular national pastime, warns that the nation's public health will not be good, and brings confusion and discord to religious issues and the churches.

The planet ruling the midheaven, also as usual, is the significator of the national government. With Libra on the midheaven, Venus has that role, and Venus is also very well dignified in this chart; she is in her day triplicity and also in one of her faces, she is placed in an angular house, and she is trine the Moon; furthermore, she is a little over 10 degrees from the Sun and thus not combust, though some astrologers would consider her to be "under sunbeams"—a minor debility, though, in this setting, a significant one.

Venus in the 7th house also indicates successful foreign relations and an active policy of establishing alliances abroad. Conjunct Jupiter, Venus indicates that the national government will have considerable wealth at its disposal, though that wealth may be disposed of too freely—as history shows. Moon trine Venus is another very strong indication of national prosperity and is a particular sign of agricultural abundance. Thus the ruler of the national government is trine the Moon, the significator of the political classes; conjunct Jupiter, the significator of the people as a whole, as ruler of the 1st; and influenced by the Sun, the significator of the presidency. That promises a history full of freewheeling political conflict in which who gets to control the executive branch and the machinery of government is the major point at issue.

The Sun, of course, deserves close attention in any mundane chart, since it rules the head of the nation's government—in the current case, the president. The Sun is in very mixed dignity in this chart. He is strengthened by placement in the angular 7th house and by the conjunction with Jupiter, but he is peregrine and afflicted by a sesquisquare with the Moon and a close applying square with Saturn. The sesquisquare with the Moon is a minor aspect, but it has more influence than usual because the Sun is in Cancer, the sign the Moon rules. Relations between the president and the country's political class will therefore be difficult more often than not. The Sun's square with Saturn is considerably more troublesome, guaranteeing that the presidency will be a difficult, grueling job, and that US presidents will by and large have a much-harder time getting their agendas enacted than the heads of most governments.

The Moon is similarly mixed in dignity. She receives a minor dignity by placement in the third face of Aquarius, and considerably more from trines with Venus and Mars, but she is in the cadent 3rd house and afflicted by sesquisquares with both ends of the Sun-Saturn square. This aspect pattern—a square aspect between two planets, each of which is sesquisquare with a third planet—was named "Thor's hammer" by astrologer Alice Portman, and it deserves the name; it's a difficult, explosive pattern associated in natal astrology with willfulness, acting out, hostile criticism from others, and disruptive behavior overturning collective norms. In a foundation chart, it clearly means the same thing.

Placed in the 3rd house, the house of transport, the Moon accurately predicts the American obsession with movement, the lure of the open road and the massive cultural importance of transport technologies—first canals, then railroads, and finally highways—in shaping the American character. In a natal chart, the Moon in the 3rd indicates someone who has trouble settling down in any one place for long, and the same is true of the US population as a whole. It also indicates in advance the role that public schooling came to play in American life, since the 3rd is the house of basic education, and it hints at the immense importance of US media worldwide during the nation's twentieth-century heyday.

Portman points out that a "Thor's hammer" pattern is somewhat less disruptive when at least one of the planets has a helpful aspect to vent some of the pressure, however, and this chart is well supplied with those; Saturn has a trine with Uranus to take off some of the pressure, while the Moon is provided with trines to Venus and Mars for the same purpose. All these are in, or conjunct the cusp of, the 7th house of foreign policy—an indication in advance of the way that domestic political stresses in the US have so often driven adventurism overseas.

Let's take a closer look next at the seventh house, with no fewer than five of the nine planets either placed in it or conjunct its cusp. We've already discussed the Sun and Jupiter. In the 7th, both of these stress the role of foreign relations and alliances in the power and prosperity of the United States, and the Sun's placement here shows the important role that foreign policy and war would play in strengthening the office of the presidency. Venus and Mars in this house, both trine the Moon, show that the crucial role of foreign relations includes both peaceful and warlike dimensions. The United States was fated to be successful in peace and war—the angular placement of both planets and the powerful assistance both receive from the trine with the Moon show this clearly enough.

These two planets, however, differ in dignity. Mars is peregrine in Gemini, while Venus is dignified by triplicity and face. Venus has wholly favorable aspects—the trine with the Moon and a conjunction with Jupiter—while Mars is afflicted by an applying square with Neptune. Thus the consequences of peace will tend to be wholly beneficial to the United States, while the consequences of war will be a very mixed bag. That Mars square Neptune is particularly problematic, since it places the United States in opposition to popular movements abroad and makes the US military prone to place too much faith in its own propaganda. This will tend to produce reliable blowback and bring considerable trouble on the country.

Uranus in this chart is in the 6th house of public health, the military, and the workforce, but he is close enough to the cusp of the 7th that he influences that house as well. Here we see the United States' role as an essentially disruptive force in global politics, and also a force for disruption and change in military affairs—an amplification of the indications of Thor's hammer. It's no accident that the United States remains the only nation to use nuclear weapons in war.

Notice also that Mercury rules the cusp of the 7th house and is located in the 8th. Mercury in this chart is peregrine, retrograde, and semisquare Uranus, though he receives some help from a sextile with Neptune. The general profile of US foreign policy is that it's well-meaning and idealistic (Mercury sextile Neptune) but phenomenally clueless (Mercury retrograde and peregrine) and prone to sudden eccentricities and unpredictable changes that cause more trouble than they solve. Mercury semisquare Uranus is very clearly expressed here.

Neptune in the 9th is another important indication. Neptune in this placement is not well dignified: in her detriment in Virgo, intercepted, in a cadent house, and afflicted by a square with Mars. What help she gets from her sextile with Mercury hardly matters by contrast. Since the 9th house rules religion and the judiciary, we can see in this placement the importance of religion in American public life, but also the pervasive tendency of American religious movements to be dragged down by schism, scandal, and fraud. Equally, this shows the soaring idealism that shapes the American concept of the law, and the profoundly flawed and often-dysfunctional ways that this idealism has expressed itself across American history.

All in all, it's a fine portrayal of the United States as the last two and a half centuries have shown it: an extraordinarily rich, restless, clueless, and conflicted nation playing an outsized role on the global stage, constantly veering back and forth between high ideals and low practices, grand plans and inept performances, and headed eventually toward an abrupt unraveling. How much of this Ebenezer Sibly foresaw is anyone's guess, since he didn't write a delineation of the chart he published in encoded form. How much of it we still have to witness before that sudden fall—well, here again, that's anyone's guess.

CASE STUDY 5

THE GRAND MUTATIONS OF 1425 AND 1663

The predictions included in the third part of this book include a discussion of one of the great astrological events of recent history, the grand mutation that took place on December 21, 2020. In order to understand it and gauge what effects it will have for the following two centuries, a glance back over several previous grand mutations may be helpful. Before the 2020 event, the most-recent grand mutations were in 1841, 1663, and 1425. The grand mutation on February 14, 1425, has certain remarkable similarities to the one in our time, and we have the advantage of knowing how things worked out in the 238 years between this and the following grand mutation in 1663.

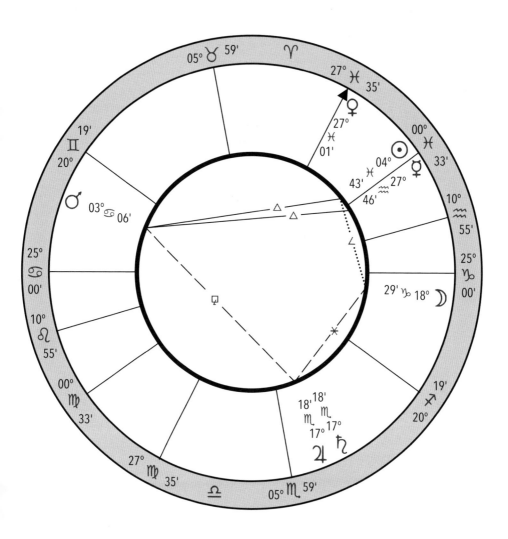

The grand mutation of 1425 in London

The grand mutation in 1425, which took place in Scorpio, marked the end of an Air cycle and the beginning of a Water cycle. In the usual way of things, the cycle of conjunctions had dipped briefly into Water earlier—there was a conjunction in Scorpio in 1305 and another in 1365, just as the Air cycle we have now entered was foreshadowed by a triple conjunction in Libra in 1980 and 1981. The 1425 event was also a triple conjunction, with February 14, March 18, and August 26 all seeing conjunctions of Jupiter and Saturn in Scorpio.

The first of these is considered far and away the most important and is the one that will be interpreted here. I have used the chart for London simply for the sake of convenience; the specific effects on each country of the grand mutation in 1425, like those of the one in 2020, depend on the chart cast at the moment of the grand mutation for that country's capital. A number of general considerations, however, can be extracted from the chart in general, and those can be compared with historical events between 1425 and 1663 to help clarify the meanings of the astrological indications. This is especially useful just now because, as already noted, the 1425 mutation has some close similarities to the 2020 chart.

Please note that I have interpreted only those planets that were known at the time of the grand mutation. According to the astrological teachings I find most valid, the discovery of each new planet or minor body represents the activation of a previously unmanifest potential in humanity's collective life.

We can begin with the Sun. The Sun in any mundane chart indicates the government, and its placement and aspects tell much about how governments will fare in the period and locality indicated by the chart. The Sun in the 1425 chart is of mildly favorable dignity; while peregrine, he is strengthened by a conjunction with an equally peregrine Mercury and by a trine with Mars in his fall in Cancer and is hindered by aspect only by a weak semisquare with the Moon in her detriment in Capricorn. More generally, though the Sun has only modest dignity, only one planet—Venus—is in better condition, and the others range from neutral to very weak. During the period when this chart applies, central governments could thus be expected to succeed through the exhaustion of their opponents.

This is exactly what happened in much of the world during the period ruled by this chart. In Britain, the Wars of the Roses ended in 1485 after the battle of Bosworth, when the exhaustion of the contending noble houses enabled the Tudors to establish a centralized government; the English civil war of 1641–45 simply settled which class would rule the government thus established. On the other end of Eurasia, in Japan, the Sengoku Jidai (Age of Warring States) ended at the battle of Sekigahara in 1600, after which the exhaustion of the contending noble houses enabled the Tokugawa shogunate to impose a similar peace on Japan. The rapid spread of the Ottoman Empire after the Battle of Chaldiran in 1514, the founding of the

Mughal Empire in India by Babur in 1526, the founding of the Russian Empire by Ivan the Terrible in 1547, and the conquest of China by the Manchus beginning in 1618 are other expressions of the same pattern.

Similar events took place in the New World during the same period: the founding of the Hodenosaunee (Iroquois) League around 1425, ending the era of confusion in northeastern North America that followed the fall of the Hopewell culture; the founding of the Aztec Empire in 1430, ending the era of confusion in Mexico that followed the fall of the Toltec Empire; and the founding of the Inca Empire in 1438 by Pachacuti Inca, ending the era of confusion in the Andean countries that followed the fall of the Wari state, all are good examples. In one of the ironies that history is full of, following the discovery of the New World in 1492, the latter two empires collapsed under the catastrophic impact of European diseases and invasion, and the resulting power vacuum was immediately filled by the Spanish Empire.

The Moon in this chart is in very mixed shape. It is in its detriment in Capricorn and suffers from a semisquare aspect with the Sun; it is strengthened, however, by a favorable sextile aspect with the Jupiter-Saturn conjunction itself. Moon semisquare Sun warns of discord between the government and powerful classes in society, with riots, uprisings, insurrections, and outright civil wars likely to occur; as noted below, this influence was also amplified by a negative aspect between Mars and Saturn. A mere list of the domestic conflicts and civil wars that took place between 1425 and 1663 would fill several pages. Since the semisquare is a minor aspect, most of these uprisings failed to accomplish much, and in many cases—as in the English civil war of 1641–45 and the French Wars of Religion from 1562 to 1598—the results gained by the winning side of the struggle turned out to be temporary and were reversed by political actions later on.

Moon sextile Jupiter is very favorable for foreign trade, for shipping, and for travel; it predicts a general increase in prosperity for the common people, especially through commerce. This also took place. The immense expansion of trade that followed the European voyages of discovery in the late 1400s and early 1500s transformed the economies of most of the world's nations and brought about drastic changes in the lives of most people. Standards of living for ordinary people rose in many parts of the world, though other changes—the slave trade above all else—plunged whole populations into misery.

Moon sextile Saturn is beneficial for agriculture, building, and public administration. During this period, food crops not previously known to the Old World—especially potatoes and maize—brought significant improvements in diet across Europe and some parts of Asia. The achievements in building during this period will be discussed later in relation to the arts, but changes in public administration were significant over most of the world's urban societies. From England, where the Tudor government laid the foundations

149

of a centralized postfeudal state, through the Ottoman and Mughal Empires, where conquests were followed by the deployment of new and, for the most part, better systems of justice and administration, to Japan, where the Tokugawn shoguns replaced decadent imperial bureaucracies with more-effective systems, and across the Pacific to the Inca Empire, which used knotted-rope quipus to maintain a level of record keeping many literate societies never managed, the growth of efficient civil services was nearly a worldwide phenomenon.

Mars, the planet of war, is in his fall in Cancer and thus appears in his most-destructive forms. The English Wars of the Roses, the French Wars of Religion, the Thirty Years' War in Germany, the brutal civil wars that brought down the Ming dynasty in China, the Sengoku Jidai in Japan—these are only the most widely known conflicts of a bitter age of wars. Mars in this chart is trine the Sun, showing the importance of warfare as a driving force in the rise of the great empires of the age. He is also trine Mercury. Until the discovery of Uranus in 1781, Mercury was the planet of technological innovation—note the way that technological innovation shifted into overdrive once it passed into the hands of the newly discovered planet of revolutionary change—and the period between 1425 and 1663 was in fact a period of dramatic technological innovation in warfare. Gunpowder, little more than a curiosity at the beginning of the period, ruled the battlefield at the end of it.

The Battle of Cerignola in 1503 was the first battle in history won by musketry; the military use of the musket was taken up so enthusiastically by the Ottoman, Persian Safavid, and Mughal Empires that these are commonly called the "Muslim gunpowder empires" by Western historians. By 1548, the revolution had spread to Japan, where the army of Takeda Shingen, the most powerful of the daimyo at that time, was crushed by Murakami Yoshikiyo's musketeers at the Battle of Uedahara. Mars in this chart is sesquisquare the Jupiter-Saturn conjunction. Mars in a negative aspect with Jupiter predicts religious dissensions and conflicts, and those duly occurred. The Reformation and Counter-Reformation in Europe, which pitted Protestant and Catholic powers against one another in a set of intermittent but brutal wars that lasted beyond the end of this period, was only one of a series of savage religious conflicts that shaped much of the history of the age.

In the Muslim world, bitter struggles between Sunni and Shi'a sects routinely ended in warfare and massacre; in India, bitter religious strife between Muslim and Hindu communities continued until it was brought to a temporary halt by the Mughal emperor Akbar the Great in 1562; in the island kingdoms of southeast Asia, religious strife worsened the conflicts between Catholic Portuguese colonizers and Muslim indigenous nations. Mars in a negative aspect with Saturn, in turn, reinforces the implications of the Moon semisquare Sun referenced above, bringing about unrest, rioting, assassinations, and civil strife.

The one really bright spot in this chart is Venus, the planet of culture and the arts in mundane astrology. At the time of this grand mutation, she was in Pisces, the sign of her exaltation, and in charts for European nations she was also the most elevated planet—that is, closer to the midheaven than any other planet known at that time. Thus it comes as no surprise that the period covered by this grand mutation was one of history's great periods of culture and the arts. In Europe it included the zenith of the Italian Renaissance, the explosive spread of Renaissance culture throughout Europe, and the first half of the baroque period as well.

During this period, Western oil painting reached its maturity, classical architecture was revived, and opera and many other musical genres were born; during this period, Leonardo da Vinci, Michelangelo, Dürer, Cervantes, and Shakespeare flourished, to cite just a few of the most famous names. This same wave of artistic and cultural creativity can be traced around the globe. During this period, Muslim architecture reached its zenith, and so did the monumental architecture and sculpture of the Aztecs. In Japan, woodblock printing became one of the fine arts, and the kabuki theater was born. In Africa, the city of Timbuktu became a major center of arts and culture.

Thus it's fair to say that the 1425 grand mutation chart does a very respectable job of predicting the broad trends at work in the 238 years that followed. While the traditional zodiacal rulerships of countries do not appear to offer useful guidance, the standard mundane meanings of the planetary locations and aspects closely match the events that followed this grand mutation. Since there are specific similarities between this chart and the 2020 grand mutation chart—the Sun in both is conjunct Mercury, in hostile aspect to the Moon, and in trine with a planet of disruptive force. Mars in 1425, Uranus in 2020, while the Moon in both is sextile to Jupiter and Saturn—those indications may be worth careful study.

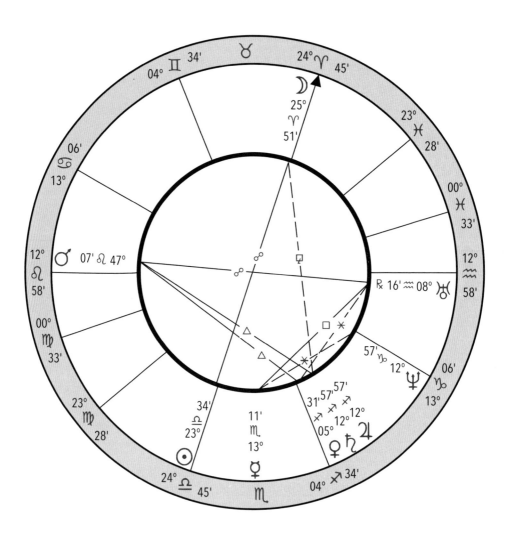

The grand mutation of 1663 in London

The grand mutation on October 16, 1663, and the 179-year cycle of the element of Fire that followed takes the story forward to 1842 and, in the process, makes it possible to glimpse something of the inner side of an important era in global history. The grand mutation in 1663, which took place in Sagittarius, marked the end of a Water cycle and the beginning of a Fire cycle. In the usual way of things, the cycle of conjunctions had dipped briefly into Fire earlier—there was a conjunction in Sagittarius in 1603 and one in Leo in 1623, just as the Air cycle we are about to enter was foreshadowed by a triple conjunction in Libra in 1980 and 1981.

The period between 1663 and 1842 is of astrological importance for another reason: for the first time in more than five thousand years, the range of planets known to humanity expanded during this period, with the discovery of Uranus in 1781; Neptune was not discovered until 1846, but its existence was successfully predicted by astronomers before the end of the era, so I have included it in this analysis. Here again, the discovery of each new planet or minor body represents the activation of a previously unmanifest potential in humanity's collective life, and the influences of these two distant planets began to play a significant role in the period governed by this chart.

We can begin examining the chart with the Moon, which dominates both this and the 1842 chart, standing alone in the heavens and opposing the Sun. Having the luminaries in opposition in these charts makes perfect sense, since the eras ruled by these two grand mutations were the great periods of democratic revolution in world history—and democracy in practice, as distinct from theory, is a system of government in which the political class as a whole exercises power directly, rather than handing it over to a monarch or the like.

This is all the more striking because the era governed by the 1663 grand mutation began as an age of powerful monarchs. The Manchu, Mughal, and Ottoman Empires dominated the Old World, and the newly founded Spanish Empire dominated the New World. On one end of Eurasia, Louis XIV of France, the "Sun King," extended his power over a Europe still shaken by the Thirty Years' War, while on the other, the early Tokugawa shoguns did exactly the same thing in a Japan still shaken by the last bitter years of the Sengoku Jidai.

By the end of the era, by contrast, those monarchies that still existed were shadows of their former selves. Revolutions in the New World swept away half of British America and nearly all of the Spanish Empire, replacing them with independent nations; France had outlasted three monarchies and was about to get rid of a fourth; the Manchu and Ottoman Empires had been reduced to client states of European colonial interests; and the Mughal Empire had been erased and replaced by the British Raj. Only the Tokugawa shogunate clung to a tenuous independence in Japan and would be overthrown shortly after the era ended.

This process is shown clearly by the Sun's position in the chart. The Sun is in his fall in Libra, and the opposition with the Moon is the only aspect shown. The lack of connection with other planets in the chart suggests the way that, during the era governed by this grand mutation, royal courts tended to become fatally detached from the realities of the societies they were supposed to govern; the Versailles syndrome, as one may as well call it, was a repeating feature in the politics of the age.

The 1663 chart drawn up for London, in fact, shows the Moon conjunct the midheaven and the Sun conjunct the nadir—not surprisingly, since the 1663 mutation is poised in between the execution of Charles I by Parliament in 1649 and the overthrow of James II by Parliament in 1688, the two acts by which royal absolutism became a thing of the past in Britain. The same chart drawn up for Philadelphia or Boston shows the Moon low in the eastern sky, having just risen above the American colonies, and Taurus—the sign of the Moon's exaltation—on the ascendant; meanwhile, the Sun of royalty has just set in the west. Looking at this chart, it's easy to see the Age of Revolutions about to dawn.

The Moon, however, is not in good condition in this chart. She is peregrine in Aries, having no natural dignity in that sign, and she is also afflicted by two aspects—the opposition with the Sun already noted, and a sesquisquare with the grand mutation itself. Moon opposite Sun shows popular dissatisfaction with government and predicts social turmoil and unrest; Moon sesquisquare Jupiter brings trouble, confusion, scandal, and extravagance to institutions and religious bodies; Moon sesquisquare Saturn brings economic troubles and general disorder in the affairs of state, as well as the deaths of officials. The point being made is clear: during the era ruled by this mutation, democratic governments can take power—and they can also crash and burn. The history of the era shows that process repeatedly in various parts of the world.

In this chart, Jupiter and Saturn are conjunct in Sagittarius, Jupiter's own sign, so the energies of the mutation work primarily through Jovian functions such as expansion, bureaucratic government, and the pursuit of profit. It's entirely appropriate that the period in which this chart was effective saw the most spectacular age of imperial expansion and conquest in recorded history, as fleets and armies poured out of Europe to conquer most of the rest of the world and carve it up into a patchwork of sprawling colonial empires. This was not a peaceful process—Mars is trine the grand mutation, making war a standard instrument of expansion. At the same time, Sagittarius is the sign of liberty and idealism and points up this era's place in history as an age of great reforms and moral crusades.

Let's take a closer look at the aspects, which show this same divergence. Mars trine Jupiter is favorable for charitable and humanitarian causes; thus it's not at all surprising that such moral issues as opposition to slavery and the first stirrings of feminism became major issues during this era. According to the old textbooks, this aspect also indicates increased attention to matters of public health and sanitation, and it's notable that both of these received serious government concern for the first time in much of the world during the period covered by this chart.

Mars trine Saturn, on the other hand, gives strength and success to governments and especially to their armies and navies. This was also a central theme of the period governed by this chart—the rise, in much of the world, of disciplined regular armies and navies under the control of central governments, in place of the more diffuse and poorly organized arrangements common before this era. Those nations that made this transition, outside Europe as well as within it, had the strength and success promised by the aspect—usually at the expense of those that did not.

The grand mutation is also in a loose applying conjunction with Venus. Venus conjunct Jupiter is another indication of idealism and public benevolence and suggests improvements in the legal and social status of women. Venus conjunct Saturn is a much more difficult aspect, predicting economic crises, the disruption of social and family life, and additional burdens on the social status of women. Ironically, all these indications are correct, since idealism and benevolence ran headfirst into the challenges imposed by difficult times, and the legal status of women veered up and down sharply with social changes.

Venus is also the planet of the fine arts, and her conjunction here can be read as an indicator of the social importance of the arts during this era. In the 1425 chart, Venus was in her exaltation; here, by contrast, she is peregrine and conjunct Jupiter and Saturn. The former aspect ushered in the Renaissance in Europe and comparable events elsewhere in the world; as this chart takes effect, the extraordinary achievements of that earlier era give way to creative ventures less potent and more subject to the zeitgeist. The world of Shakespeare, Rembrandt, and Bashō gives way to the world of Austen, Canaletto, and Utamaro. Only in music does a golden age follow—most of the truly great achievements of baroque, classical, and Romantic music in Europe happen during this era.

The planet of war is an active presence in this chart. Though he is peregrine in Leo, he has four aspects, all of them applying and three of them positive; war is therefore a major feature of the period. Since Mars is in Leo and is therefore ruled by the Sun and is in opposition to Uranus, the planet of freedom, a good many of the wars in question were launched by monarchs in an attempt to crush democratic movements—a strategy that often backfired fatally, as in the Revolutionary War in America and the first round of European wars that followed the French Revolution. Notice also the applying trine between Mars and the grand mutation: no matter who won any given war, the act of making war itself tended to push things further along the track laid out by the mutation itself. Alongside his other aspects,

Mars is trine Venus in this chart. In mundane astrology this is an indication of an increased birthrate and points up one of the most important trends of the era: the beginning of the steep increase in sheer human numbers, which has reached its peak in our time.

Mercury, the planet of mind and language, is a more significant influence in this chart than he seems at first glance. While he is peregrine in Scorpio, he makes aspects to Uranus and Neptune, the newly discovered planets that govern influences from outside time. Mercury square Uranus shows the traumatic process whereby traditional ideas about the universe were shredded by new scientific discoveries, which are ruled by Uranus; Mercury sextile Neptune shows the transformation of literature and thought that was set in motion by the discovery of the ordinary person, one of Neptune's rulerships as a subject for poetry and prose. Whereas Shakespeare wrote of the doings of kings in his plays, Austen recounted the everyday lives of men and women in her novels: that shift had immense consequences in the era that followed.

Notice how Neptune's only aspect is with Mercury—only among writers and other intellectuals had the first stirrings of the new planetary influence become evident before the next grand mutation. Uranus, by contrast, is an active force in the chart. He opposes Mars, indicating the dramatic role played by new technology. One of his rulerships in rendering the old art of war obsolete; he squares Mercury, with effects already indicated; and he sextiles Venus—this shows not only the significant influence of new technologies and discoveries on the arts during this period, but also the rise of the cult of the artist as individual. The artists of the Renaissance had thought of themselves as craftspeople, trained via the usual route of apprenticeship and honored for their technical skills; over the course of the era this chart covers, artists came to be honored instead for the uniqueness of their vision, a Uranian theme.

As with the 1425 chart, it's fair to say that this chart does a good job of tracing out at least some of the essential historical trends of the period it covers. Very few of the trends marked out in this chart are also found in the upcoming 2020 grand mutation, however—the conflict between Moon and Sun. Opposition in 1663 and square in 2020 is the only significant parallel— and so this chart and the era it heralded should be seen in contrast to the era the world entered on December 21, 2020.

CASE STUDY 6

ZADKIEL'S LEGACY

In examining the next grand mutation, in 1842, we have an unusual resource: a work by a major astrologer discussing the mutation and making specific predictions on its basis. *Zadkiel's Legacy*, published in 1842, attempted to predict the future on the basis of that year's grand mutation. It was written by Richard Morrison, one of the premier astrologers of the time, under his pen name Zadkiel and may be accessed online free of charge at www.archive.org and various other websites. The *Legacy* is written in the high-flown style standard for astrological writings of early Victorian vintage, but it is worth reading, and I encourage students of mundane astrology to download it and follow Morrison's logic.

What I propose to do here is go through Zadkiel's predictions and see how he did. We'll score +1 for each accurate prediction, −1 for each inaccurate prediction, 0 for each partly right and partly wrong prediction or each trivial prediction, +2 for each really striking success, and −2 for each total flop.

1. *Great moral and political changes in the condition of the people, brought about by sudden and violent revolutions* (p. 6). He was wrong about Britain, which managed to get through the period without a violent revolution, but this prediction was based on the zodiacal location of Jupiter and Saturn and thus applies to the whole world. As a prediction for the world, however, it was spot on—the period between 1842 and 2020 saw an unusually large number of revolutions that brought about major changes in society. Score: 0.

2. *Britain will adopt a policy of appeasing foreign enemies by cash payments* (p. 6). He was right about the appeasement, particularly in the 1930s, but wrong about the cash payments. Score: 0.

3. *Great and serious detriment to Britain by means of foreign loans* (p. 7). Square on target; the financial crises that hammered Britain in relation to the war debt for the two world wars are only the high points of a long history of foreign-exchange crises. Score: 2.

4. *Significant decrease in the influence and authority of the church, the aristocracy, judges, and lawyers* (p. 7). True in the first two cases, not true in the second two. The scale of the loss of authority on the part of the Church of England and the British aristocracy between 1842 and 2020 was all but unimaginable in Zadkiel's time; while judges and lawyers avoided any significant loss of power, he deserves partial credit. Score: 1.

5. *Disastrous floods causing great economic harm* (pp. 7–8). Correct but trivial; those have been common enough in British history. Score: 0.

6. *Attacks on British commerce and shipping by enemy powers* (p. 7). That turned out to be a feature of both world wars, since German U-boats came close to starving Britain by cutting off the trade that kept its population fed. Score: 1.

7. *Massive increases in taxation will burden the people* (pp. 8 and 9). He certainly called that one. Score: 2.

8. *Increased luxury, extravagance, and the enthusiastic pursuit of vices* (p. 8). As far as I know, this has been a feature of every age, but several periods of British history between 1842 and 2020—the Edwardian era, the Roaring Twenties, and the 1960s—were especially notable for these. Score: 1.

9. *The merchants and tradesmen of Britain will flourish, especially those in the western half of the country* (p. 8). In 1842, Britain was the world's dominant economic power, with direct or indirect control of most global trade, and that status remained in place until after the First World War. In the wake of the Second World War, however, Britain's economy went into a tailspin from which it has never really recovered. Score: 0.

10. *The property of the Church of England will be devoted to the purposes of the state* (p. 9). A near miss. Between 1842 and 2020 the Church of England lost what control it still had of its property and revenue, and the government took charge of it but did not devote it to political purposes. Score: 0.

11. *Government deficits caused by protracted wars and public health will become a massive economic burden to the British people* (p. 9). This was square on target. Score: 1.

12. *Epidemics of cholera will cause financial distress to the nation* (p. 9). A partial hit. Britain suffered several severe cholera epidemics over the course of the nineteenth century, but their economic impact was not that significant. Score: 0.

13. *Sudden quarrels and disputes with neighboring countries, especially Portugal* (pp. 10 and 20). He was certainly right about the quarrels and disputes, but wrong about the country. Germany was still a congeries of little states in 1842, however, and so Zadkiel would have had to be unusually clear-sighted—more so than anyone else in his time—to foresee the coming of the German Empire or the Third Reich. Score: 0.

14. *Railways will be replaced by other modes of conveyance not yet thought of* (p. 10). Zadkiel was not quite correct that the railways would be entirely replaced, but he was right that new modes of transport were on their way, which would take over much of the traffic that in 1842 went by rail. Score: 1.

15. *Important improvements to the agricultural economy through new roads, new modes of transport, and discoveries and inventions of a chemical nature* (p. 10). As far as I know, nobody else in 1842 predicted the invention of chemical fertilizers and pesticides, much less the explosive spread of paved roads through Britain that was such a striking feature of its twentieth-century history. Zadkiel's vision here was astonishingly precise. Score: 2.

16. *Property values will rise to unprecedented levels* (p. 10). This was correct. Score: 1.

17. *The British mining industry will be very successful, and many new mines will be opened* (p. 11). Another solid hit. Score: 1.

18. *Class warfare will be a pervasive feature of the era ahead and will result in the eventual victory of the working classes as a result of pestilence and the death of many of the rich* (pp. 11–12). Zadkiel was correct that the struggle between the rich and the poor would be a defining feature of British life during the period ruled by this grand mutation, and he was correct that the victory of the working classes would be as a result of matters belonging to the 8th house. The 8th house, however, rules inheritance as well as death, and as many British people alive today remember, the thing that eventually decided the struggle was the steep increase in death duties under Labour governments, which siphoned off the concentration of wealth in the hands of the rich and made the rise of a social welfare state possible. Score: 1.

19. *The British theater can expect a golden age, with many famous and successful plays being written and produced* (p. 12). Here, of course, he was quite correct. Score: 1.

20. *There will be many bad harvests until 1851, but better harvests after that date* (p. 12). He was right on the first count but wrong on the second. Score: 0.

21. *Laws restricting the importation of grain to Britain will be repealed around 1858, resulting in much less hunger and misery for the poor* (pp. 12–13). He was right

about the policy but off a bit about the timing; the repeal of the Corn Laws took effect in 1850. Still, he was close. Score: 1.

22. *After 1851, educational reforms will result in a much-higher level of public education* (p. 13). Here he was quite correct, since the system of publicly funded schools was one of the great triumphs of the second half of the century. Score: 1.

23. *A serious epidemic will afflict London in 1875* (p. 13). No such epidemic happened. Score: −2.

24. *Britain's naval forces will suffer a defeat in battle in 1875 due to the treachery of an ally* (p. 14). A flat miss on this one, since nothing of the sort happened. Score: −2.

25. *A more popular form of religious worship will become widespread after 1850* (p. 14). The Low Church movement in the Anglican Church and a variety of dissenting Protestant denominations became much more widespread after this year, so this counts as a hit. Score: 1.

26. *Much of the commerce of England will migrate to India* (p. 15). This was a significant economic issue in the second half of the nineteenth century, as British entrepreneurs moved their manufacturing plants to India to take advantage of cheap labor, driving down wages in Britain. Score: 1.

27. *There will be dramatic changes in methods of naval warfare and the introduction of new weapons and technologies, but their introduction will involve a great deal of bloodshed and heavy expenditures* (p. 16). A remarkably good hit by Zadkiel. Score: 2.

28. *Britain faces many major wars during the period of this mutation, and many battles will be fought by British troops in North Africa* (p. 16). And another. Score: 2.

29. *Britain will fight a great naval war against America and Egypt* (p. 16). This one, on the other hand, was a genuine dud. In 1842 the United States and Britain were hostile nations, having fought two fierce wars within living memory; the Anglo-American alliance that dominated the history of the twentieth century was nowhere on the political horizon yet, and the stars do not seem to have helped Zadkiel anticipate it. Score: −2.

30. *Britain will fight a major war in India against the Russians* (p. 16). Another complete flop. Many people expected this, but of course it never happened. Score: −2.

31. *Epidemic fevers will be a major cause of death in Britain during the period of this mutation* (p. 17). True but trivial, since epidemic illnesses causing fever were a major cause of death all over the world until the twentieth century. Score: 0.

32. *British Christianity will move away from Puritanism and strict Sabbath keeping in order to focus on personal spirituality and charitable works* (p. 18). A solid hit. Score: 1.

33. *A spectacular era of scientific and technological innovation is about to dawn, which will bring dramatic economic changes and partly relieve the difficulties of the poor* (p. 18). Accurate, but there were people beginning to predict this in Zadkiel's time. Score: 1.

34. *England will take the lead in this scientific and technological leap forward* (p. 18). Another hit; Britain was the most important center of innovation until the Second World War. Score: 1.

35. *An abundant new energy resource will largely replace coal-fired steam engines and will probably have to do with windpower* (p. 19). An abundant new energy resource was indeed discovered, but it was petroleum, not wind. Score: 0.

36. *Queen Victoria will not survive the period of influence of the lunar eclipse of May 21, 1845, and thereafter a bad monarch will reign until he is driven out by a revolution* (p. 20). Zadkiel veils this prediction in symbolic language, which, however, isn't hard to interpret. This was a complete flop; Victoria outlived the effects of the eclipse for more than half a century. Score: −2.

37. *The cost of naval expenditures will become a massive burden to the British government* (p. 21). This was of course quite correct. Score: 1.

38. *Dramatic changes to the power and influence of the House of Lords* (p. 21). Another correct prediction. Score: 1.

39. *By the time the period of the mutation is half complete, people will look back on the treatment of the poor in 1842 as inhuman and barbaric* (p. 22). The period was half over in 1931, and of course this is quite correct. Score: 1.

40. *Effective relief for the working poor will come only as a result of labor organization* (p. 22). That's certainly what history shows. Score: 1.

41. *British rule in India will end and a new Indian government emerge, after long struggles and sufferings* (p. 23). Another correct prediction. Score: 1.

42. *A new religion will arise in India* (p. 24). Several have arisen, but none with the exact characteristics he describes. Score: 0.

43. *A great spiritual leader will appear in India; one result of his activities will be bloodshed on a large scale* (p. 24). Here, on the other hand, Zadkiel is strikingly correct. Gandhi's leadership in the struggle for Indian independence was of course successful, but the aftermath involved large-scale struggles between Hindu and Muslim populations and a very large number of deaths. Score: 2.

44. *India will suffer terrible earthquakes* (p. 24). True but trivial, since India sits on a major tectonically active region. Score: 0.

45. *Very important changes will take place in the government of India in 1853 and 1861* (p. 24). A very, very near miss! Dramatic changes followed the Indian Mutiny of 1857–58. We'll be generous and give him this one. Score: 1.

46. *India will be devastated by pestilence, flooding, and earthquakes in the summer of 1871* (pp. 24–25). This, on the other hand, was a thorough flop. Score: −2.

47. *The great spiritual leader predicted above will arise soon after 1871 and will win followers all through India and Afghanistan* (p. 25). Um, no. Score: −2.

48. *Conspiracies, plots, and insurrections against the British rulers of India will be an ongoing theme throughout the period of the mutation. They will succeed eventually, after many years, in establishing a representative government in India* (p. 26). An exact and correct prediction. Score: 2.

49. *The commerce, trade, and revenue of India will undergo great changes as India becomes a major manufacturing power* (p. 26). Correct. Score: 1.

50: *Naval warfare will rage along the coasts and rivers of India* (p. 26). This, on the other hand, didn't happen. Score: −1.

51. *A member of the royal house of Saxony will die around 1845* (p. 27). True but trivial; it was a large family. Score: 0.

52. *Great changes are in store for the people of Germany* (p. 28). Correct if vague. Score: 1.

53. *Floods and famine will cause much suffering in Saxony in 1842* (p. 28). This was correct, though the worst years of the "Hungry Forties" were later in the decade. Score: 1.

54. *Severe earthquakes will afflict Mexico* (p. 29). True but trivial; like India, Mexico is in a tectonically active zone. Score: 0.

55. *The government of Mexico will soon be overthrown, and its independence is seriously threatened* (p. 29). True on all counts. The US war with Mexico, followed by the French conquest of Mexico and the installation of Maximilian I as emperor of Mexico, followed by the resurgence of American hegemony over its southern neighbor once the Civil War was over, were important features of the era. Score: 2.

56. *A catalogue of earthquakes expected in different places and dates in the mid-19th century* (pp. 29–30). Zadkiel thought he could predict earthquakes with astrology, and he was incorrect. Since this is something of a sideline from his main set of predictions, I'm going to lump them in together as one giant flop. Score: −2.

All told, Zadkiel comes out well ahead. His total for successful predictions amounts to 41 points; subtract a score of 17 for his failed predictions and he still comes out well to the positive side. Furthermore, of his 14 predictions that were partly true and partly false, or true but trivial, the great majority got at least some details right.

We can draw some definite conclusions from this survey. The first is that mundane charts based on the cycle of grand mutations do seem to offer accurate information about general trends for the period ruled by a mutation. Those of Zadkiel's forecasts that were most stunningly prescient—the reshaping of the British landscape by paved roads, new transport technologies, and agricultural chemicals, for example, or the huge economic burden that new naval warfare technologies would place on the British government— were broad general trends. They were certainly specific enough to be a basis for action—for example, an investor who read *Zadkiel's Legacy* in the decades after 1842 and decided to go long on shares in naval-armaments firms, say, would have done very well—but they did not deal with specific individuals and dates.

Conversely, mundane charts based on the cycle of grand mutations are very poor predictors of specific events affecting specific people or appearing on specific dates. All of Zadkiel's really embarrassing flops came when he attempted to make detailed predictions of events assigned to specific years. There are astrological methods that are effective for this purpose, but grand mutation charts do not seem to be among them.

Furthermore, the traditional symbolism that assigns zodiacal signs to countries produces very mixed predictions in these charts. When Zadkiel insisted that Britain would fight a naval war against Egypt and America, and that Portugal would be an important enemy of Britain, he was basing this on the old system that attributed signs to countries. On the other hand, this pointed him to Britain's military involvement in North Africa and to a highly prescient survey of Mexico's future. More research will need to be done to determine where these attributions are and are not useful.

Finally, Zadkiel's method of predicting earthquakes by astrology doesn't work. It was doubtless worth a try, and Zadkiel had the courage to put his predictions out there to be tested, but the results are in and the test came back negative. It may be that some other method will allow this to be done, but Zadkiel's method can be ruled out.

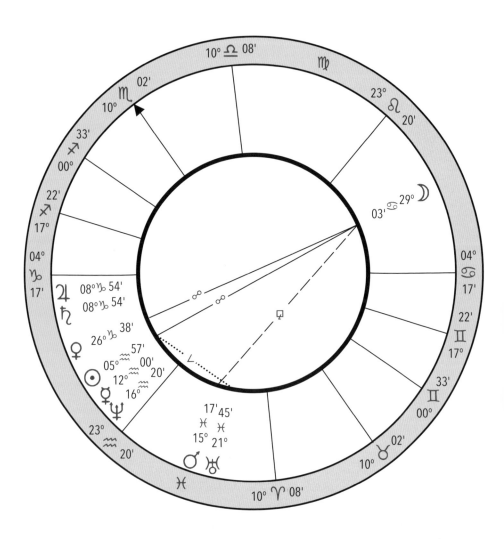

The grand mutation of 1842 in London

Looking back on the 1842 grand mutation with the benefit of hindsight, the following points stand out to me. In this chart the Moon is the most influential planetary factor, in her rulership in Cancer and standing by herself, while the other planets crowd into less than a quarter of the zodiac. The Moon stands opposite the Sun, but no other planet rivals her; only Saturn is of equal strength, and his only aspect is the conjunction he makes with Jupiter.

The Moon in mundane astrology is the planet of the common people of a nation, and more specifically that portion of the population that takes an active role in the political and cultural discourse of the time. In this chart, it is the planet of democracy, and its dominant position in this chart predicted the most dramatic transformation in global politics in this period: the spread of democratic forms of government to most of the world's nations. It's important to remember, in this context, that "democratic" does not mean "utopian"; history shows that nations that elect their leaders by some form of popular vote—which in the final analysis is all that "democratic" means— are perfectly capable of invading their neighbors, abusing minorities, and tolerating injustices. Even so, an era when a perfectly ordinary hereditary monarchy like North Korea insists on calling itself a Democratic People's Republic is something highly unusual in world history.

The Sun is the planet of government, and traditionally it is above all the planet of monarchy. The opposition in this chart between Moon and Sun is thus a massive factor in the period ruled by this grand mutation. The Sun is in his detriment in Aquarius, the Moon in her rulership in Cancer, so the conflict between them will normally have just one outcome. This is mirrored precisely in the history of the world between 1842 and 2020. In 1842, most of the countries on earth were ruled by monarchs: a quarter of the Earth's land surface was under the British Crown, while the czar of Russia; the emperors of China, Persia, and the Austro-Hungarian Empire; and any number of mere kings accounted for much of the remainder. In 2020, monarchs are an endangered species, and most of those that remain are purely ornamental. This is unprecedented in world history, but then I know of no previous grand mutation in which the Moon has had so dominant a position in the chart.

The Moon is also opposite Venus, the planet of culture and the arts, which is dignified in her day triplicity, meaning that she has dignity in charts only when the Sun is above the horizon. From Europe across the Atlantic to the western edges of North America, the Sun is below the horizon and Venus is therefore without strength. Here again, it's not at all difficult to interpret this in terms of the events of the following 178 years. During that time, in the countries where Venus had no dignity, an astonishing gap opened up between the artistic and cultural community, on the one hand, and the populace, on the other. Before 1842, it was unthinkable that artists would despise the public and go out of their way to create works that offended and excluded as many people as possible. As the influences of the grand mutation came into play, however, this is exactly what happened across the Western world.

Finally, the Moon is sesquisquare Mars, the planet of war, who is dignified in his night triplicity and conjunct Uranus, the planet of technology. The conflict between the Moon and Mars—or, to put things in political terms, between democratic regimes and military dictatorships—has been a recurring theme between 1842 and 2020, especially in the half of the world where the Sun was below the horizon at the time of the mutation: all of Europe, the western half of Africa, and the entire Western Hemisphere. The tendencies for democratic popular movements to be in favor of peace, and for coups carried out by the military to be the usual way that fragile democracies collapse, reflect the same Moon-Mars aspect.

Meanwhile, both the radical transformation of war by technology and the dramatic advances in technology driven by war are shown by the conjunction between Mars and Uranus. Notice here also how Uranus, but not Mars, is semisquare the Sun; this shows the way that technological change has tended to destabilize existing governmental institutions during the period covered by this chart.

In mundane-astrology charts, Mercury is usually in conjunction with the Sun, reflecting the tendency of every society's educational system and communications media to say what governments tell them to say. The 1663 chart was an anomaly in this regard, with Mercury far from the Sun and making important aspects with Uranus and Neptune; this showed the dramatic decentralizing impact of widespread literacy and rapidly proliferating print technology on society in the late seventh and eighteenth centuries. In this chart, Mercury has returned to conjunction with the Sun, but it is a loose and separating conjunction—as weak as a conjunction can be—and he is also in a closer, applying conjunction with Neptune, the planet of mass movements and mass phenomena, such as fashions and fads.

It's hard to think of a better way to represent, in astrological terms, the way that education and the communications media have become mass phenomena, reaching out to far-larger audiences than ever before but more subservient than ever before to the vagaries of popular taste and fashion, and the tangled relationship between educational institutions and media conglomerates, on the one hand, and central governments, on the other. The first half of that equation began to emerge in the wake of the 1663 grand mutation, when Mercury was in a close sextile to Neptune, and a great many writers about media and education tend to take it as an unchangeable fact. As we'll see, though, it does not exist in the 2020 grand mutation chart, and we can therefore expect significant shifts in education and communications as the influences of this mutation begin to take effect.

The possibility that the age of universal public education and fad-driven mass media may be drawing to its close should be seriously considered.

In this chart, Jupiter and Saturn are conjunct in Capricorn. That placement gives Saturn great strength, since Capricorn is the sign of his rulership, but it makes Jupiter weak because Capricorn is the sign of his fall. While the way this combination works out will vary from place to place depending on the local chart, great strength to the Greater Malefic and great weakness to the Greater Benefic did not augur well for the era that began with this aspect. Of course, history does not contradict that judgment; the period from 1842 to 2020 includes so many of the most destructive wars and worst genocides in human history, along with a bumper crop of famines, economic depressions, and other sources of human misery.

At the same time, unlike any of the other charts we've considered or will be considering, this chart has the Jupiter-Saturn conjunction making no aspects to any other planet. Existing theoretical material on mundane astrology doesn't provide a specific meaning for this, but an analogy with other forms of astrology may be worth exploring. An ingress chart in which important planets are unrelated to the rest of the chart predicts a period dominated by events that are not subject to anyone's control. It may not be accidental, in other words, that the era now ending is superlatively the era in which history happened to people, rather than being made by them. Sudden dislocations in which events spun out of control and had consequences no one predicted in advance have been very common over the last 178 years. In the era that follows the 2020 grand mutation, that may be less common.

More generally, this chart has remarkably few aspects. The theoretical material on mundane astrology I've studied doesn't draw an explicit connection between this pattern and the monolithic power blocs in permanent conflict that make up so much of the history of the last 178 years, but it may be worth further research to see if the assortment of aspects in a grand mutation chart corresponds to the character of the era that the grand mutation ushers in.

PART 3

PREDICTIONS

THE GRAND MUTATION
OF 2020

On December 21, 2020, the world passed into a new period of its history, a cycle of Air signs that will remain in place until 2219. This grand mutation thus has a period of effect of 199 years, during which time its effects will be modified by other great conjunctions at roughly twenty-year intervals. Since the grand mutation also functions as an ordinary great conjunction between Jupiter and Saturn, its effects will be felt with particular strength during the twenty-year period between December 21, 2020, and the next Jupiter-Saturn conjunction on October 31, 2040.

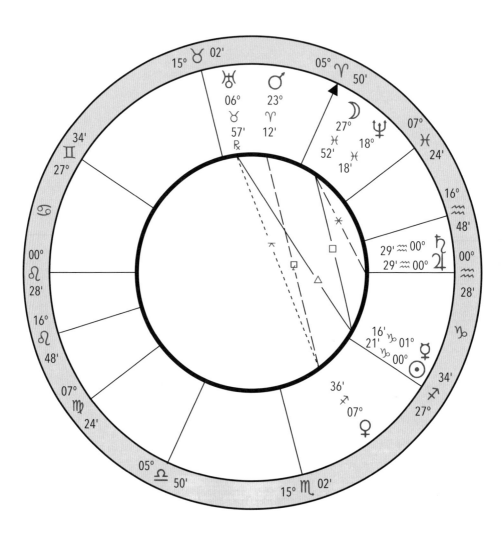

The grand mutation of 2020 in London

The effects of the grand conjunction are strongest when angular—that is, in the 1st, 4th, 7th, or 10th houses. The conjunction is in the 1st house in the middle of the Pacific Ocean, affecting only a few islands, but the 4th-house placement includes China and Thailand, the 7th-house placement includes England and Spain, and the 10th house, the strongest of all, includes Canada and the United States. The specific effects of the conjunction depend, as always, on the details of the chart for each nation. Certain broad trends can, however, be determined from the dignities and aspects of the planets at the time of the conjunction.

In this chart, two planets, Mars and Neptune, are in their rulerships; one, Uranus, is in his fall; none of the others receive any important dignity or debility from their placement by sign. In general—and of course, like every other indication of the grand mutation, these will vary according to the indications of the chart specific to each nation—war and religion will be strengthened during the period of effect of this chart, while technology will face significant troubles, all the more because Uranus is also the sole retrograde planet in this chart.

The Sun in a mundane chart indicates the government of a nation, the Moon indicates the nation's people, and a square aspect between the two luminaries foretells discord, conflict, and disruptions between governments and people. Under this aspect, discontent tends to be widespread, and the actions and policies of governments tend to be unpopular. The next two hundred years, and the next twenty in particular, will thus see more than the usual amount of political unrest and agitation, especially in those countries ruled by Aquarius, or in which the conjunction is angular.

The period about to dawn has very close similarities to the one defined by the 1425 grand mutation in Scorpio, which like the 2020 chart had Sun and Moon in a hostile aspect; the Sun strengthened by a conjunction with Mercury and a trine with a malefic (in that case), Mars, and the Moon strengthened by a sextile with the conjunction between Jupiter and Saturn. The Sun-Moon conflict in the 2020 chart is stronger than in the 1425 chart, and the Moon was in its detriment in 1425, while she suffers no such disadvantage in 2020. The conflict between Sun and Moon, government and people, will thus involve less warfare than in 1425–1663, when the Sun was trine Mars, and it will also be less one-sided; governments, however powerful, will have to treat popular unrest and disapproval as forces to be reckoned with.

The Sun is strengthened in these conflicts by a close conjunction with Mercury and an applying trine aspect with Uranus. Mercury conjunct Sun furthers intellectual, scientific, and literary movements; improvements to education; and new legislation; it can also indicate important developments in technology. Sun trine Uranus, the planet of radical change, brings important reforms that strengthen the government and its head. It predicts new legislation, increased force and vigor in the national life, and success at home and abroad. Wherever either the Sun or Uranus is angular, this combination of aspects predicts significant changes in laws and constitutions to strengthen the power of the executive branch of government. Thus we can expect to see governments in many parts of the world strengthened in the twenty years immediately ahead.

More broadly, the next two centuries will be an era of political centralization, similar to the age of powerful monarchies that extended from the 1425 grand mutation in Scorpio to the 1663 grand mutation in Sagittarius—an era that, as noted earlier, saw the Spanish Empire in Europe and the New World, the Mughal Empire in India, and the Manchu Empire in China reach their zenith; the establishment of the Aztec and Inca Empires and the Hodenosaunee (Iroquois) League in the Americas; and the end of long periods of political and social chaos in Japan and Britain with the restoration of strong central governments under the Tokugawas and Tudors, respectively. Which countries will be most strongly influenced by this set of patterns, again, must be determined from national charts for the grand mutation.

The Moon is almost as strongly placed in the conflicts mentioned above as the Sun. In place of the Mercury conjunction and Uranus trine supporting the Sun, it receives the potent support of an applying sextile aspect with the Jupiter-Saturn conjunction itself, though it also suffers from a square with Mercury. Moon sextile Jupiter is fortunate for business and trade and indicates that prosperity will spread fairly widely among the general population. Moon sextile Saturn is very favorable for agriculture, forestry, and other land-based agricultural sectors and is also fortunate for national finances. It brings domestic tranquility and encourages economic stability. All these factors will tend to strengthen the position of the people vis-à-vis the governmental power indicated by the Sun: it is one of the commonplaces of political history that governments gain power through crisis and lose it through prolonged peace.

Moon square Mercury partly undoes the stabilizing influence of Moon sextile Saturn, however. It predicts controversies in national life, disputes in national legislatures, and trouble in foreign affairs. Since Mercury has an influence on technology, it also indicates that technology will prove unexpectedly unstable and troublesome, with a range of failures and unwelcome side effects that will cause widespread problems over the period covered by this chart. To the extent that governments become identified with national technological infrastructures, problems with technology will tend to feed the conflict between governments and peoples.

Among the other implications of these aspects are that the more extreme end of climate-change forecasts will turn out to be inaccurate, and that the predictions of a drastic economic crisis in the near future are also unlikely to pan out. There will certainly be economic crises in the two centuries covered by this grand mutation chart, as in every period of comparable length, but the indications are that they will be somewhat less frequent and severe than the crises in the period of 1842–2020 covered by the last grand mutation. Equally, though, rosy predictions of ongoing technological progress that fail to pay attention to the downsides of new technology will prove to be embarrassingly shortsighted.

The applying trine aspect between Mercury and Uranus also bears on the future of technology. Uranus rules science and industrialism—the discovery of Uranus in 1781 marked the beginning of the great transformation of European economies from an agrarian to an industrial basis, and it also marked the point at which science stopped being the hobby of a privileged elite and turned into a significant cultural and economic force in its own right. Mercury rules communication, information, and education. In the 2020 chart, however, both planets are in troubled conditions; Mercury has no dignity in Capricorn and is combust—too close to the Sun and thus weakened by its overwhelming presence—while Uranus is retrograde and in its fall in Taurus.

Taken together with the Moon square Mercury discussed earlier, this suggests that the two centuries ahead will see the downsides of science, technology, and industrialism highlighted by events. Uranus retrograde suggests that a significant number of technological advances will be given up or lost over that period. The trines between Uranus and Mercury and the Sun, respectively, however, indicate that remedial measures are available. One way to read this would be to suggest that prompt and effective government responses to technological disasters will be among the factors that strengthen the trend toward political centralization indicated by other factors in the chart.

Venus, finally, is the planet governing culture, literature, and the arts in a mundane chart, and we have seen already that her fortunes in the grand mutations of the past correlate closely with the ups and downs of culture during the cycles that followed. The 1425 chart had Venus exalted in Pisces and trine Neptune, showing the extraordinary flowering of the arts and culture in the late Renaissance and early baroque eras that followed; the 1663 chart had Venus neutrally dignified in Sagittarius but benefited by an applying conjunction with the Jupiter-Saturn conjunction itself, announcing the immense cultural importance of the artistic ventures that followed, including the classical eras of European music and painting, the heyday of woodblock prints and the golden age of Kabuki theater in Japan, and parallel ventures in other societies. The 1842 chart, by contrast, had Venus neutrally dignified in Capricorn and afflicted by an opposition with an extremely strong Moon, announcing the turn of popular taste away from the arts and culture (Moon opposite Venus) and the coming of an era of hackneyed and heavily commercialized art (Venus in Capricorn).

The 2020 chart has Venus neutrally dignified in Sagittarius, suffering only minor negative aspects from Mars and Uranus. Art and culture are therefore likely to fare somewhat better over the next two centuries than they did in the schlock-art era that began in 1842. The ongoing troubles with technology will hinder the flourishing of artistic, literary, and cultural movements (Uranus retrograde and in fall inconjunct Venus from her own sign), and difficulties due to wars and civil unrest will also plague the new cultural ventures of the next 199 years (Mars in Aries sesquisquare Venus). However, the hostility between the arts community and the public that dominated culture in the wake of the 1842 grand mutation will no longer be an issue, and Venus's placement in Sagittarius suggests a turn away from the heavy commercialization of art and culture, and toward something like the aspirations that guided the arts between 1663 and 1842, when the governing chart also had Venus in Sagittarius.

THE ISLAMIC EMIRATE
OF AFGHANISTAN

As many people noticed, Francis Fukuyama's famously silly claim that history stopped during the first Bush administration got another hard disproof in the summer of 2021, as the puppet government in Afghanistan installed by the US got brushed aside with contemptuous ease by the Taliban militias, resulting in one of the more embarrassing foreign-policy fiascoes of recent American and world history. On August 19, the Taliban duly proclaimed the Islamic Emirate of Afghanistan; the available sources indicate that this happened around noon, which is enough detail to allow a foundation chart to be cast.

As discussed earlier in this book, the date and time at which a new government is proclaimed has the same role in mundane astrology that the birth data and time of an individual has in natal astrology. From the foundation chart, it is possible to judge something of the character and destiny of the government. The one difference is that it's not easy to choose when you are born, but governments can choose when they get proclaimed. If they happen to be founded in a part of the world where astrology is commonly practiced, and have the common sense to consult a competent astrologer, they can elect a time for the proclamation of the new government that will give it the best possible start in life.

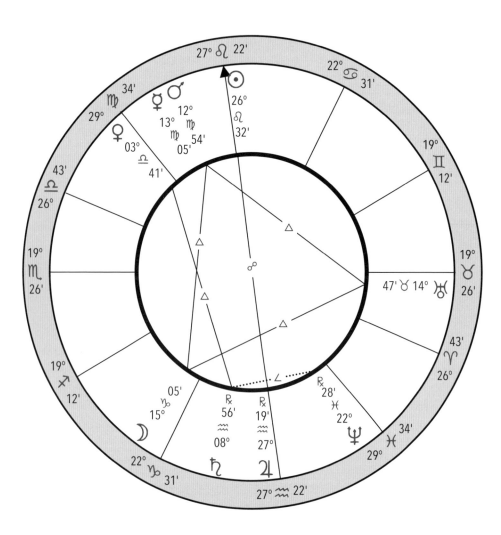

The foundation chart of the Islamic Emirate of Afghanistan on Aug. 19, 2021

This the Taliban apparently did. The Muslim world has a long and very rich astrological history, Afghanistan is well stocked with learned astrologers, and one of them seems to have put some serious work into choosing the time and date for the proclamation. Let's go through this chart step by step and see what the Taliban's astrologer worked out for them.

First in importance for any government is the condition of the Sun and the 10th house, since the first of these rules the head of state and the second rules the government in general. This chart did the sensible thing and combined the two by putting the Sun conjunct the midheaven. The Sun is in his rulership in Leo, and also in his day triplicity, so he is very well dignified essentially; he is conjunct the midheaven, and thus very strong (my guess is that the actual time of the proclamation was a little before noon, while the Sun was still in the 10th house and therefore angular). Sun conjunct midheaven makes the government prosperous and popular and brings good fortune to the country.

The one drawback with this placement is that the Sun is opposite Jupiter. It's a strong opposition; since Jupiter is retrograde, both planets are moving toward each other, a condition called mutual application. Sun opposite Jupiter disturbs trade and commerce, guarantees religious disputes, and predicts scandal and trouble involving members of the government. Why did the astrologer choose a date that had this problem? Because other factors were important enough to outweigh that, and you have to take what you can get from the heavens. One of the great challenges in electional astrology is that you can never get a perfect chart, and so you do your best and warn your clients what to watch for (we'll discuss what to watch for in Afghan politics and society a little later on in this exploration).

So the Sun is in about the best possible position for a new government. Let's go on to the other factors affecting the 10th house. Two planets, Mars and Mercury, are very closely conjunct in that house. Mercury is in his exaltation in Virgo; Mars is dignified by mixed triplicity in the same sign; both, of course, are in an angular house and therefore strong, and as we'll see, both receive considerable help from aspects. Mercury well dignified in the 10th is favorable for trade, commerce, and education, as well as for government ceremonials—including the proclamation of a new government! Mars well dignified in the 10th brings victory in war and makes the country and the government successful and strong.

Both these planets are also on the receiving end of the most favorable aspect pattern in astrology, the grand trine. The grand trine is the equilateral triangle you see dominating the chart, with Mars and Mercury at one point, the Moon at another, and Uranus at the third. A grand trine functions like an ordinary trine on steroids; it brings planetary energies into a harmonious balance and leads to calm, peaceful conditions. Mercury conjunct Mars is usually a difficult aspect, promising civil unrest and constant turmoil; with the influence of the grand trine at work, these indications are greatly minimized, suggesting that compromise between competing factions will be the order of the day.

What makes this fascinating is that all three points of the grand trine are equally troubled. The Moon is in Capricorn, the sign of her detriment, and Uranus is in Taurus, the sign of his fall. These would be seriously problematic, except that the influence of the grand trine will tend to counteract the negative influences of these planetary positions. The Moon in the 2nd house with any dignity at all is very favorable for national prosperity, and the grand trine amplifies that. Uranus in the 6th is a much more difficult placement; even when well dignified, he promises discontent and disaffection among the workforce and the military, and problems with public health; these will happen, especially in the rural regions of the country. Uranus rules the 4th house of the hinterlands, but the grand trine offers some hope of resolving them. By choosing a time when the planets were aligned in this pattern and Uranus was weakly placed in a cadent house, so that it will have less effect than otherwise, the astrologer really earned his fee.

Many people in Western countries are concerned about the status of women under the new Taliban government. The Taliban, or at least their astrologer, seem to have had that in mind as well. Venus is the planet that rules women's concerns in mundane astrology, as Mars rules men's concerns; Venus in this chart is in her rulership in Libra, and her one aspect is a trine with Saturn, thus well dignified. Expect women to be subject to traditional restrictions (Saturn is the planet of conservatism) but otherwise in a considerably less difficult position than they were under the earlier Taliban regime twenty years ago (Venus in her rulership). Since Venus is in the 11th house of legislation, expect to see laws governing women become an ongoing issue in Afghanistan under Taliban rule.

Venus also governs the 7th house of foreign policy, since the sign on the 7th-house cusp, Taurus, is ruled by Venus. Expect the new government to follow through on its promises to maintain good relations with its neighbors and to stop terrorist groups from using Afghan territory for bases (the last thing the new government wants is another twenty-year occupation by whatever foreign power decides to stomp terrorists next). Other nations wanting to trade with Afghanistan for its substantial mineral resources will be enthusiastically welcomed by the new government (the 8th house of foreign trade is ruled by Mercury well dignified in the 10th) but should be aware that ongoing instability in outlying regions will be an ongoing source of trouble (Mercury conjunct Mars). The new regime will also have an easy time getting foreign investment, with Iran, Russia, and China among the likely sources—here again, this is shown by Mercury's rulership of the 8th house.

More generally, the Taliban can be expected to pursue its conservative Muslim religious agenda, especially in the fields of communication and culture. This is shown by Saturn's placement, in and ruling the 3rd house of the media, writing, and communication. In modern astrology, Saturn is in his day triplicity in Aquarius, but in all probability the astrologer who cast this election was working with traditional assignments and thus considers Saturn to be in his rulership in Aquarius, therefore strong. He is cadent and retrograde, however, and so the ability of the Taliban to advance its cultural agenda will be more limited than it would otherwise be.

Jupiter in this chart is on the cusp of the 4th house, and if I'm correct and "around noon" means just far enough before noon that the Sun was in the 10th house, Jupiter will have been in the 4th house of agriculture and resource industries. This is where the opposition between the Sun and Jupiter may turn out to be problematic for the new government. Afghanistan has abundant reserves of commercially valuable minerals; in an era when many other supplies of these minerals are running short, this means that a great deal of money can be made by mining those minerals and selling them abroad. With Jupiter retrograde and opposing the Sun, the risk of spectacular corruption and the "resource curse" that has devastated so many other poor nations is not small. Since Jupiter is in the 4th house of the rural hinterland, the most likely source of trouble is regional warlords and tribal confederations in outlying areas cutting their own deals with foreign mining firms, evading control and taxation by the central government and weakening the national economy (Jupiter ruling the 2nd); since the Sun is so well dignified, the government will be able to push back hard, but this will be a continuing problem throughout the period of Afghan history ruled by the new emirate.

Another problem is indicated by Neptune retrograde, angular, and in his rulership in Pisces, placed in the 4th house and ruling the 5th. Neptune is, among other things, the ruler of narcotic drugs, and Afghanistan is one of the world's major growing regions for the opium poppy. During its previous era of power twenty years ago, the Taliban succeeded in stopping opium production—a detail that may have contributed to its downfall, if the long-standing rumors concerning CIA involvement in the global drug trade are correct. This time, even if the government attempts to shut down opium production, it will not succeed in doing so. The cascade of problems that unfold from the drug trade in other parts of the world that produce large quantities of narcotics will inevitably become a significant problem in Afghanistan as well. Expect drug money to spill into various corners of Afghan society, generating rapid boom-bust cycles. Neptune rules the 5th house of speculation and fueling resistance to the new government's religious and moral regulations.

These are significant problems, but the Taliban's astrologer had to work with what the heavens provided, and he did a very good job. Over the next few years, in light of this chart, I expect Afghanistan to settle down and become one more relatively ordinary central Asian Muslim nation, with pervasive but not crippling problems generated by the drug trade and by corrupt deals involving its mineral wealth, a national economy about as prosperous as a poor central Asian nation can expect, and ongoing skirmishes between the religious beliefs of its leaders and the less straitlaced notions of many of its people. I certainly hope the country experiences something along those lines; the last twenty years of corrupt US-backed governance and endless war have been very hard on the Afghan people, and they deserve a less difficult future.

THE GREAT CONJUNCTION OF 2040

The next great conjunction after the 2020 grand mutation takes place on October 31, 2040. While the grand mutation's chart will still apply after that date and will continue to apply until the next grand mutation in 2219, each great conjunction during that interval has its own influence. Thus, a look at the chart for the 2040 grand conjunction offers a glimpse at the world that today's infants will inhabit when they reach middle age.

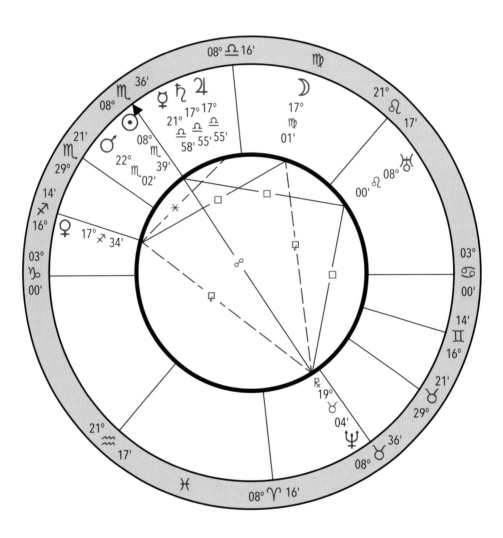

The great conjunction of 2040

The conjunction takes place in 17° Libra, and both Jupiter and Saturn are well dignified there. Jupiter in that degree of Libra is in his mixed triplicity and term, while Saturn in Libra is in his exaltation and thus very strongly dignified. Neither planet suffers from any negative aspect (aside from Jupiter's conjunction with Saturn, of course), and both planets are strengthened by a sextile with the benefic planet Venus. Venus sextile Jupiter promotes peace and goodwill, and Venus sextile a well-dignified Saturn predicts economic prosperity and stability. In any country where these planets are strong by house, despite the other indications in this chart, the twenty years following this conjunction will tend to be more peaceful, stable, and prosperous than usual.

Jupiter and Saturn are also in a loose conjunction with Mercury. In this chart, this aspect has unusual features, because Mercury ends a retrograde period the day before the great conjunction and is moving very slowly at the time of the chart—so slowly, in fact, that Jupiter is faster and is therefore technically applying to conjunction, while Mercury is separating from slow Saturn. This is relevant because an applying aspect indicates a set of conditions that can be expected to increase while a chart is in effect, while a separating aspect indicates a set of conditions that has already passed its peak and is fading out.

Mercury conjunct Jupiter is a favorable indication, good for trade and commerce as well as communication, education, and literature. Mercury conjunct Saturn is the opposite, warning of disturbances to trade and commerce, and troubled times for communication, education, and literature. In countries where these planets are strong by house, the era that begins with the grand conjunction will open as the troubles of the previous twenty years begin to fade out, while a less difficult set of conditions will be coming into play as the era proceeds.

In mundane astrology the Sun represents government and the Moon represents the people, and in particular that subset of the people of any country who are active and influential in the political sphere. In this chart, both Sun and Moon are peregrine—that is, without any essential dignity—and they are not in aspect with each other. Each of them, furthermore, is part of a different aspect pattern that places them in conflict with other planets, and the only planet these two aspect patterns have in common is Neptune, the planet of mass phenomena.

Neptune is in many ways the dominant planet in this chart. Even though he is peregrine and retrograde, he occupies one side of the chart and all the other planets in the chart are on the other, a condition that gives him unusual influence. Since he is retrograde and afflicted both by luminaries and two other planets, in turn, that influence will not be beneficial. We can therefore expect the era from 2040 to 2060 to be powerfully shaped by delusions, misunderstandings, and a widespread unwillingness to face up to the realities of the world situation.

The Sun, Uranus, and Neptune set out the most challenging combination of influences at work in this period. The Sun is opposite Neptune, and both the Sun and Neptune are square Uranus, forming the aspect pattern known as a T square. This pattern shows a three-way tug-of-war among contending forces: the Sun, which in mundane astrology represents governments; Uranus, which represents technology; and Neptune, which represents all forms of mass phenomena, including political movements and organized religion. In this conflict, none of the three forces have any essential dignity: the Sun is peregrine in Scorpio, Uranus is in his detriment in Leo, and Neptune is peregrine in Taurus and retrograde to boot. How this conflict will play out in each country will depend on which house cusps these planets rule in the grand conjunction chart for that country's capital, and how strongly it will affect the country will depend on whether any of the planets in the T square are angular or cadent.

Generally speaking, however, Sun square Uranus warns of sudden and unexpected troubles for governments, unwise legislation, bad policies, autocratic use of power, and divisions within the leadership of the nation. Sun opposite Neptune predicts unpopularity or misfortune for rulers, disorder and confusion, and general unraveling: as H. S. Green's classic text on mundane astrology notes, "Something in the nature of a downfall or collapse takes place." It can also warn of explosive scandals. Uranus square Neptune, finally, indicates political discord, trouble, and delay; attempts at great reforms that fail or provoke forceful blowback; conflict between rulers and ruled; and the fall of governments. Since the role of Uranus as the planet of technology is still being worked out by astrologers on the basis of experience, the exact place of technological change in these convulsions is not yet certain but is likely to be considerable.

Traditionally, the resolution of a T square is to be found in the sign where its missing fourth corner would be: in this chart, the point of the zodiac opposite to Uranus. This raises a fascinating point, because that fourth corner is in Aquarius, which is ruled by Uranus!

Problematic as Uranus is in this chart, the problems it indicates can be solved only by activity in its own sphere, the realm of technological change. Our current prejudices might suggest that the crisis can be solved only by technological progress, but it is just as possible that technological regress will resolve the problem, perhaps by the exhaustion of some resource or the breakdown of some technological system over which the contending forces are struggling.

Another important aspect pattern in this chart also warns of troubles ahead, though they will be of a different nature. The Moon and Venus are in square aspect, and both are sesquisquare to Neptune. As noted earlier in this book, astrologer Alice Portman has named this aspect pattern Thor's hammer. It's a good description, since it's one of those aspect patterns that can wallop you good and hard. In less symbolic terms, the conflict indicated by the square is intractable because it is held in place by the "handle," the planet to which both ends of the square are sesquisquare. In this case the conflict will be subtle rather than obvious because all three of the planets involved are peregrine and thus have no essential dignity, and Neptune is retrograde.

This aspect pattern has two main areas of impact. To begin with, it warns of great volatility in the economic sector, frequent crises and bankruptcies, and financial trouble for governments, which will face soaring expenditures and faltering tax revenues. The place of Neptune in this pattern is crucial, since Neptune is, among other things, the planet of fraud and folly, of "extraordinary popular delusions and the madness of crowds"; at the root of the economic troubles of this period, in other words, will be a failure to understand what is actually going on, because the accepted economic theories completely fail to account for what is happening or because fraud and imposture are pervasive, or both. Where one or more of the planets in this pattern are angular, expect speculative bubbles and financial fraud to play an extremely large and disruptive role in economic affairs.

The Moon and Venus are also the planets that govern human reproduction, and a square between them indicates a decline in the birthrate and the breakdown of family life. Neptune in hostile aspect to both indicates powerful cultural shifts that discourage reproduction and encourage the diversion of sexual energies away from family life. In an age of overpopulation, this is not necessarily a crisis in the short term, but it can become one in the middle to long term if the birthrate plunges far enough that the upcoming generations cannot support the economic burden of their elders—a situation that is already true in some industrial countries. So far, that has been papered over via immigration and a variety of economic gimmicks, but once the entire planet moves into depopulation, a prospect already being discussed by demographers, the fissures will become impossible to ignore.

More broadly, the Moon governs the politically influential minority among the people, Venus is the planet of culture and the arts, and Neptune is the planet of the masses. Expect a difficult three-way struggle among these factors as the influential classes turn their back on culture (Moon square Venus), and the bulk of the population has no time for either side in the resulting quarrel. Abandonment of cultural heritage by elites is of course a common feature of eras of decline. In this case, fortunately, Venus receives the benefit of a sextile with the great conjunction itself, and so time is on her side.

The one planet in this chart that is not in aspect to any other, Mars, is also the strongest planet in the chart, being strongly dignified in his rulership in Scorpio. The risk of war during the twenty-year interval governed by this chart is thus very high. Since Mars is isolated from the other planets in the chart, the wars that take place will do nothing to resolve or affect the other trends indicated in this chart, and it seems likely that none of them will lead to any significant changes in the overall trajectory of history.

This marks an interesting similarity between the current chart and the chart for 2020's grand mutation. In that chart, Mars was also in his rulership, this time in Aries, and though he was in a sesquisquare with Venus, this was his only interaction with the rest of the chart. While this indicates that wars will certainly take place between 2020 and 2040, and indeed throughout the 199-year era of history that began in 2020, it suggests that those wars will have less of an impact on society and history than current notions tend to suggest.

Interestingly, Mars in the 2040 chart is in an inconjunct aspect to Mars in the 2020 chart. This suggests that whatever changes might have been set in motion by wars between 2020 and 2040 will likely be frustrated by further wars between 2040 and 2060.

When we compare this chart more generally with the chart for 2020's grand mutation, the implications are fascinating. Every planet in the 2040 chart except the Sun is in aspect with Neptune's position in the grand mutation, and five planets in the 2040 chart also make aspects to Venus in the grand mutation; similarly, Neptune in the 2040 chart makes aspects with every planet in the grand mutation chart except for the Moon and Mars, and Venus in the 2040 chart makes aspects to four planets in the grand mutation. Sorting out all those aspects would require something closer to a book than a simple delineation, but a few points are worth extracting from the intricacies of the chart.

The first is the reaction of popular culture and collective consciousness to the changes indicated by these two charts. The events of 2040–60 will tend to frustrate changes in the popular mind that were set in motion in 2020 and will continue until 2219 (Jupiter and Saturn in 2040 inconjunct Neptune in 2020), and popular culture and collective thought in 2040–60 will tend to react by pushing back against that broader flow of events. Most likely this will take the form of efforts by people in 2040–60 to return to the state of affairs before 2020, or at least to convince themselves that they have done so or are doing so; this is also suggested by the retrograde condition of Neptune in the 2040 chart.

If the period from 2020 to 2219 turns out to be an era of technological contraction and regress, as suggested by the extremely negative condition of Uranus in the 2020 chart, the period ruled by the 2040 great conjunction will likely see sustained attempts to deny the reality of contraction. Defunct technological systems will not be rebuilt, since Uranus remains severely afflicted in this chart, but other reasons, ideological or frankly mythological, will be found to account for their abandonment. Note that Uranus in the two charts forms a square aspect with itself: the changes in technology that take place between 2020 and 2040 will be found to load additional difficulties on the technological systems that function, or fail to do so, between 2040 and 2060.

The second point that seems worth mentioning here is the intriguing relationship that Venus has between the two charts. Venus in the 2040 chart is semisquare Jupiter and Saturn in the 2020 chart, and Jupiter and Saturn in the 2040 chart are semisquare Venus in the 2020 chart! Since Venus in mundane astrology is the planet that governs culture and the arts, this suggests very strongly that the artistic and cultural movements of the period from 2020 to 2040 will be rejected wholesale by the artistic and cultural movements of the period from 2040 to 2060. Of course, this is far from unusual in the history of art—even the most-brilliant periods of creative achievement tend to be dismissed as irrelevant or unpleasant by people of the immediately following period—but the revision in taste in the current case may be rather more forceful than usual. Those readers who collect art in the years to come, if they expect it to function as a long-term investment, may need to rethink that project.

Over the longer term, ironically, the vagaries of creative fashion between these two eras will likely be seen as slight variations on a common theme. This is shown by the very similar placements of Venus in the two charts—in both cases, peregrine in Sagittarius, in a sesquisquare aspect with a malefic planet. The similarities will be visible only from the perspective of the far future, to be sure, but this also is a common event in art history.

BIBLIOGRAPHY

Bonatti, Guido. *Bonatti on Mundane Astrology*. Translated by Benjamin N. Dykes. Minneapolis: Cazimi, 2010.

Campion, Nicholas. *The Great Year: Astrology, Millennarianism, and History in the Western Tradition*. London: Arkana, 1994.

Carter, Charles E. O. *An Introduction to Political Astrology*. London: L. N. Fowler, 1969.

Goldstein-Jacobson, Ivy. *Foundation of the Astrological Chart*. Pasadena, CA: Ivy Goldstein-Jacobson, 1959.

Goldstein-Jacobson, Ivy. *The Way of Astrology*. Pasadena, CA: Ivy Goldstein-Jacobson, 1967

Green, H. S. *Mundane or National Astrology*. London: L. N. Fowler, 1911.

Greer, John Michael. *The Twilight of Pluto*. Rochester, VT: Inner Traditions, 2022.

Hickey, Isabel M. *Astrology: A Cosmic Science*. Sebastopol, CA: CRCS, 1992.

Kohout, Ed. "The Riddle of the Sibly Chart for American Independence." https:edkohout.wordpress.com/mundane/sibly-1. Accessed January 15, 2022.

Lilly, William. *An Easie and Familiar Method Whereby to Judge the Effects Depending on Eclipses, Either of the Sun or Moon*. London: H. Blunden, 1652.

Morrison, Richard. "Zadkiel." In *Zadkiel's Legacy*. London: Sherwood, 1842.

Pearce, Alfred J. *The Science of the Stars*. London: Simpkin, Marshall, 1881.

Portman, Alice. "Thor's Hammer." https:aliceportman.com/thors-hammer/. Accessed January 12, 2022.

Ramesey, William. *Astrologia Restaurata; or, Astrology Restored*. London: Robert White, 1653.

Roell, David, ed. *Mundane Astrology: The Astrology of Nations and States*. Bel Air, MD: Astrology Classics, 2004.

Smith, Robert Cross. "Raphael." In *Raphael's Mundane Astrology*. London: Foulsham, 1932.

Van Norstrand, Frederick. *Precepts in Mundane Astrology*. New York: Macoy, 1962.

INDEX

INDEX

ABOUT THE AUTHOR

Born in the gritty Navy town of Bremerton, Washington, and raised in the south Seattle suburbs, John Michael Greer began writing about as soon as he could hold a pencil. His first book, *Paths of Wisdom*, was published in 1996; since then he has authored twenty science fiction and fantasy novels and more than fifty nonfiction books on a wide range of subjects, focusing on the revival of forgotten ideas, insights, and traditions of practice from the rubbish heap of history. Along the way, he has been initiated into a variety of Masonic, Hermetic, and Druidic lineages; was consecrated as a Gnostic bishop; and turned his longtime interest in the science of the stars into a second career as a political astrologer. He lives in Rhode Island.